# Spiders and Flies

# Spiders and Flies

## Help for Parents and Teachers of Sexually Abused Children

### DONALD HILLMAN
*Burlington, Vermont, Center for Children, Youth, and Families*

### JANICE SOLEK-TEFFT
*Underhill, Vermont, School System*

Lexington Books

*D. C. Heath and Company • Lexington, Massachusetts • Toronto*

*Library of Congress Cataloging-in-Publication Data*

Hillman, Donald.
Spiders and flies : help for parents and teachers of sexually abused children /
Donald Hillman, Janice Solek-Tefft.

    p.    cm.
    Bibliography: p.
    Includes index.
    ISBN 0-669-17982-5 (alk. paper). ISBN 0-669-17983-3 (pbk. : alk. paper)
    1. Child molesting—United States. 2. Sexually abused children—
Rehabilitation—United States. I. Solek-Tefft, Janice.
II. Title.
HQ72.U53H56  1988                                   87-38062
362.7'044—dc19                                          CIP

Published simultaneously in Canada
Printed in the United States of America
Casebound International Standard Book Number: 0-669-17982-5
Paperbound International Standard Book Number: 0-669-17983-3
Library of Congress Catalog Card Number 87-46363

The paper used in this publication meets the minimum requirements of
American National Standard for Information Sciences—Permanence of
Paper for Printed Library Materials, ANSI Z39.48-1984. ∞™

    90  91  92  8  7  6  5  4

# Dedication

*To our spouses, Judith and Kenneth,*
*and to our children, Cara, Stephanie,*
*Emily, Nicole, and Gabrielle*

# Contents

# List of Tables

# Preface

T HE sexual abuse of children is a serious area of concern, with reports of such abuse steadily increasing in frequency and intensity. This book addresses the general topic of child sexual abuse and, more specifically, helpful ways of dealing with children who have experienced abuse. The book is intended for parents, teachers, and counselors who have come into contact with such children.

There has been increasing awareness of this problem, and some attention paid to the educational and prevention aspects surrounding abuse. As such, many articles and films about child safety have been developed, and several schools have adopted "personal safety" curricula, which involve in part a focus on ways of preventing abuse. For example, distinctions are made between "good touching" and "bad touching," personal and interpersonal matters, and between "private" and "public" parts of one's body. Though these attempts at addressing sexual abuse are extremely important, the primary emphasis has been on helping children gain more *awareness* of the problem, and to develop behaviors that will prevent or minimize abusive episodes. Unfortunately, many children have been, or will be, abused, regardless of awareness or prevention training. This book, *Spiders and Flies*, is aimed at giving parents, teachers, and counselors a set of concrete skills to use when they suspect or discover that a child has been abused. A summary of key prevention ideas are included as well, to be used for both abused and non-abused children so that future abusive occurrences could be dealt with successfully. We have also written a companion book intended for abused children themselves to use, providing information, awareness, and a number of concrete activities that the child can perform.

As child clinicians, both of us have been involved with child sexual abuse cases in many ways, as therapists, as teachers, as evaluators, and as expert witnesses in legal proceedings. We have conducted numerous workshops for teachers and counselors, and have spoken with many parents about this topic. The ideas for *Spiders and Flies* stem from these activities, and have been strongly suggested and supported by all groups, especially so by parents and teachers whose lives have been affected by this ordeal. We hope that the ideas and strategies described in the book will prove equally valuable and useful to others.

# Acknowledgments

G RATEFUL appreciation is expressed to Jo Ann Hernandez for permission to use her sensitive and meaningful poems concerning her traumatic history. We also are indebted to the many children and parents with whom we have worked. Their suffering, struggle, and courage have helped our understanding immeasurably and touched our lives.

Our participation on the Chittenden County Sexual Response Team over the past six years has provided us with much stimulation, information, and informed discussion. This book stemmed from community outreach efforts initiated by the team.

We also wish to thank the many professionals with whom we discussed cases and issues, and from whom we received helpful information. Planned Parenthood of Northern New England was particularly helpful in sharing their knowledge of resources. Thanks also go to our marvelous typist, Audry Racine, for her dedication and diligence to the many manuscript changes, and to the staff at Lexington Books from whom we received much support. Lastly, we want to acknowledge the patient support and understanding we have received from our families throughout this process. It is to them that the book is lovingly dedicated.

# 1

# Background

C HILD sexual abuse is perhaps the most unreported crime in the country at this time.* Various surveys indicate approximately 25 percent of Americans have been victims of child sexual abuse. In addition, an increasing number of children who are both victims and offenders is being reported.

If the definition of abuse is slightly expanded to include any offensive or intrusive sexual behavior perpetrated on another person, it is probable that almost all people at one time or another have been victims of an offensive sexual attack or advance. Considering the magnitude of this problem, it is remarkable that so little information and help concerning sexual misbehavior is available. Recently, however, attempts at increasing public and professional awareness in terms of prevention, diagnosis, and treatment of sexual abuse, particularly in regard to children, have been made. Several prevention projects are now available on film, videotape, and filmstrip and in books and other educational programs. In addition, more physicians, nurses, and mental health professionals are receiving training in the diagnosis and treatment of sexual abuse. But little information is available to parents and families, particularly in terms of dealing with the aftermath of reported sexual abuse. The aim of this book is to provide parents and teachers of sexually abused children with specific strategies they can use to help alleviate stress and improve coping skills both for them-

---

*For the purposes of this book, the word *child* will refer to anyone from birth to eighteen years old. Thus, adolescents are certainly included.

selves and the child. The book also reviews several important concepts related to prevention, although specific details of formal prevention programs are not included.

## Definition

In general, child sexual abuse is defined as the utilization or exploitation of a child by an adult, adolescent, or older child for sexual purposes. Specific actions and behaviors must, of course, be viewed in terms of intention, context, and culture. In general, however, sexual abuse presumes a child's voluntary or involuntary participation in actions about which he or she has little understanding and thus there is no possibility of informed consent. Such involvement typically evokes significant psychological or physical damage, both acute and long lasting.

## Types

There are many types of sexual abuse, depending on the nature of the actions involved, particularly whether there is direct physical or sexual bodily contact.

### *Physical Contact Sexual Offenses*

Incest—sexual relations within a family involving a parent or sibling and a child

Rape—sexual relations involving an adult who is not a member of the family and a child

Prostitution—the use or sale of a child for sexual purposes intended for economic gain

Pornography—the use or sale of depictions of a child engaged in sexual activities intended for economic gain

### *Nontouching Sexual Offenses*

Verbal abuse—the overexposure of a child to sexual language and descriptions about which he or she has little understanding and which serves to cause emotional distress

Exhibitionism—sexual exposure of some kind (usually by an adult to a child intended to shock or frighten the child)

Voyeurism—observation of sexual, genital or excretionary actions or nudity of a child by an adolescent or adult

Primal scene—direct exposure of a child to adults having sexual relations without appropriate processing or discussion with the child

All these types of abuse entail a wide variety of actions, ranging from mildly intrusive sexual teasing or play to much more provocative and assaultive sexual contact involving a high degree of manipulation, threat, or force. Thus, one child might report that her uncle liked to rub and pat her "bottom," while another child might reveal that he has been the unwilling victim of anal intercourse in a situation involving force. The majority of sexual abuse offenses, however, appear to entail subtle means of coercion. They begin with more innocent activities and only gradually become increasingly perverse and exploitive. Most sexual abuse also is perpetrated by people whom the victim knows, often a close friend or family member. Once again, such misbehavior is often masked by a variety of other, more normal activities present in day-to-day living.

## Myths about Sexual Abuse

*Sexual abuse is typically perpetrated by strangers (the stranger/danger myth).* From several investigations, it appears that the majority of sexual abuse cases are perpetrated by people extremely familiar to the victim, most often a person with whom the victim has extensive contact as well as a significant relationship. It has been found that 75 to

80 percent of sexual abuse occurs within so-called affinity systems (Kempe and Kempe 1984).

*Sexual offenders are monsters, perverts, or dirty old men in raincoats.* The majority of offenders are physically nondescript and appear to be quite normal in most areas of functioning (Groth 1979; Russell 1986).

*Child molesters are always male.* Although the majority of offenders who have been discovered are male, female offenders represent a significant minority. About 5 percent of sexual abuse of girls and 20 percent of sexual abuse of boys is perpetrated by older females (Finkelhor 1984). Further, many examples of subtle sexual abuse perpetrated by women might be masked as displays of affection, as such behavior is more acceptable for women in this culture. Thus, victims are more likely to report assaults by males, as there often is less confusion about the nature of the action and the violation that occurred.

*Girls are the only targets of sexual abuse.* In the past few years, the percentage of molestation reported by boys has increased significantly, particularly in preschool and latency years. Since 1980 the percentage of male sexual victims increased at a greater rate than that of female victims. Closer examination reveals nearly equal victimization, particularly in early and middle childhood years. Overall incidence rates, however, still suggest that girls are victimized two or three times more often than boys (Russell 1986). On the other hand, since the majority of offenders are men, sexual abuse of boys frequently constitutes a type of homosexual experience that most victims are even more hesitant to disclose. Also, boys tend to be less emotionally expressive than girls, particularly in talking about their feelings and experiences. Instead, boys tend to act out their distress in various problematic ways. About 80 percent of child molesters (largely male) were themselves abused as children (Freeman-Longo 1985) and most confirmed child molesters (pedophiles) prefer young males.

*Many children fantasize or lie about sexual abuse.* Although children occasionally think and wonder about sex, they rarely fantasize about being abused in any way. It is also extremely rare that children ever lie about sexual abuse (Sgroi 1982).

*Abuse victims usually play a seductive and provocative part—that is, they often "ask for it."* Children rarely play an instrumental part in abuse, as genital sexuality is simply not a motivating factor during most of childhood. Even when it is (in adolescence, for example), sexual interest is mainly directed toward peers. For the most part, children have little or no conception of sex and are thus in no way able to give informed consent to such actions (MacFarlane et al. 1986).

*Homosexual adults are significant threats to become child molesters.* Sexual abuse is not related to sexual orientation. Most offenders, even of same sex victims, are heterosexual and have no conscious homosexual desires, interests, or behavior patterns (Groth 1979).

*The best way to deal with sexual abuse is to forget about it and put it out of your mind.* Many adult survivors seem to have incorporated this myth, attempting to repress the negative experience they encountered. Unfortunately, such a direction poses serious emotional problems, both at the time of the abuse and over the years. It is crucial that victims work through the trauma of sexual abuse in an expressive manner (Burgess et al. 1978; Butler 1978; Mrazek et al. 1981).

*Incest is an acceptable way of learning about sex in some families.* Even in the rare cases where incestuous experience is known and condoned by the adults in the family, incest breaks major psychological, generational, family, moral, and legal boundaries. It also affects many areas of development and socialization. Adults who employ such arguments are mainly thinking of their own gratification and not of the welfare of the children involved (Justice and Justice 1979; Meiselman 1978).

*Sexual abuse is sexually motivated.* Motives for sexual abuse are quite complicated, typically a mixture of power and affection as primary needs. Sexuality, though often present to some degree, is a secondary motive (Brownmiller 1975).

*Sexual abuse of young children is a new phenomenon, caused by an erosion of morals.* Although there has been a vast increase in the number of sexual abuse cases reported, all evidence suggests that the percentage of children being sexually abused is no greater at this time than at previous times. On one hand, there is considerable suspicion that incest might have been more prevalent in earlier periods, when children were expected to be completely submissive to the demands and whims of their parents. On the other hand, systems of morality were more strictly delineated in the past, with harsher consequences of breaking those rules. Thus, it is impossible to gauge the magnitude of sexual abuse accurately over the course of history, although it is clear that such abuse is not a new phenomenon (Rush 1980).

*Most cases of sexual abuse are reported.* While the number of reported sexual abuse cases is growing at a significant rate, there appears to be a considerable number of unreported cases. It has been estimated that only between 20 and 50 percent of abuse cases are reported to authorities (Kempe and Kempe 1984). Failure to report seems to occur for a variety of reasons, including fear, ignorance, guilt, embarrassment, and suppression.

## Incidence and Prevalence

Generally, it is estimated that one in three children will be sexually abused by age eighteen (Russell 1986). Conservative estimates predict that nearly 40 percent of girls and 30 percent of boys will be abused during their childhood. A nationwide study of child molestation provides a typical example of these findings (*Los Angeles Times*, August 25, 1985). In this study, 2,627 adults across the country were chosen randomly and surveyed over the telephone. The authors reported the following results:

> More than 22 percent of the total stated that they were definitely sexually abused.

> Twenty-seven percent of the women surveyed and 16 percent of the men surveyed stated that they had been molested as children.

Sexual intercourse was involved in 55 percent of the molestations; 36 percent had been fondled; 7 percent were confronted by exhibitionists; and 1 percent were sodomized.

The majority of molestations were isolated incidents, but 39 percent of the victims of intercourse reported repeated abuse (in six cases lasting more than ten years).

Ninety-three percent of the abusers were males.

Approximately two-thirds of the victims were girls.

The most vulnerable age was about ten.

Abusers were about twenty years older than their victims.

Forty-one percent of the abusers were considered to be friends and acquaintances, 27 percent strangers, and 23 percent relatives.

About half the abusers were considered to be people in authority over the victim.

Only 18 percent of the victims said they were forced to participate. Victims often stated, however, that they were manipulated or subtly pressured to comply.

Generally, the victims' motives were a combination of fear, anxiety, confusion, and submission. Motives for the abusers (according to the victims) included mental illness, loneliness, homosexuality, and alcoholism.

Sixteen percent of the victims said the molester did not believe that his or her actions were wrong.

Victims were not more likely to come from lower socioeconomic or particular ethnic groups.

Victims did not exhibit higher criminal behavior.

Victims reported only slightly less happy childhoods and family closeness than nonvictims.

Signficantly more victims felt that their childhood sex education was inadequate.

Fewer than half the victims told someone (usually a parent, other relative, or friend) about being molested within a year after the incident. Only 3 percent reported the incident to the police or another public agency. One in three of the victims said that they had never told anyone about the molestation until the survey itself, chiefly because they were afraid, ashamed, or did not consider the event to be serious.

Seven out of ten who did inform someone about the abuse said that no effective action was taken.

More than half the victims and 47 percent of the general public agreed with the statement, "Sexual assault within families is very common."

These results are not sensationalized. In fact, they probably are only minimum estimates of the actual abuse that occurs in all classes, races, sexes, ages, and neighborhoods. Preliminary studies in other countries also suggest that child sexual abuse is not unique to the United States but that it is a worldwide problem. Although estimates vary slightly, the general conclusion in the United States is that one in every three girls and one in every six boys is sexually abused before the age of eighteen (Russell 1986). Based on a total U.S. child population of approximately 60 million children, this would imply that more than 500,000 new cases of sexual abuse occur each year. It also has been estimated that about 300,000 children are involved in prostitution and pornography (Kempe and Kempe 1984). Despite these staggering totals, actual reports of sexual abuse suggest that it is frequently unreported, particularly to authorities. There are signs of change in recent years, however, presumably due to greater public and professional awareness of domestic violence, child abuse, sexual boundaries and children's rights in general.

In fact, reports of sexual abuse have increased significantly within recent years, up approximately 200 percent since 1976 (Kempe and Kempe 1984). Again, it is unclear whether this represents a greater frequency of reporting or a greater frequency of abuse, although tentative findings suggest that more of the effect is due to increased awareness of abuse and acceptance of disclosure. Although numbers of reported cases have been increasing significantly over the past ten years, it appears that most cases are never reported to the authorities.

When victims do inform about their abuse, more than half of the victims directly tell an adult, usually someone in the family. And even if they do not tell someone directly, the telltale signs of abuse are often evident to people who know the child well. Thus parents and teachers often appear to know about the abuse or at least should know that something has happened (or is happening) to a child. It is a crucial duty to become more aware of sexual abuse, to report cases to the appropriate authorities, and to assist the child in working through the ordeal. The rest of this book provides the rationale and guidelines for such action.

# 2

# Normal Sexual Development

A LTHOUGH this book focuses on sexual abuse and its remediation, it is important to review normal sexual development and related feelings, behaviors, and interactions. It is only when the range of normal behavior is violated that abnormal behavior is evident.

Before describing various stages of growth, it should be noted that sexual normality and abnormality are highly ethical matters in most cultures and certainly in Judeo-Christian cultures. The resulting ethical precepts that follow from various religious denominations within this general framework are not always in accord with behaviors "normally" occurring in nonproblematic children. This discrepancy sometimes produces a great deal of tension, particularly if the ethical persuasion is to deny or denigrate any evidence or display of sexuality (at least before marraige).

Yet another problem occurs in the changing norms and morals concerning sexuality, changes seen quite vividly in American culture over the past three decades. Formerly negative views regarding premarital sex, birth control, divorce, homosexuality, serial marriages, and unmarried couples living together are now viewed as more acceptable (and sometimes quite positive) lifestyles. Because of these considerations, any account of "normal" sexual development is subject to intense criticism. What follows is a summary of behaviors displayed, feelings experienced, ideas expressed, and bodily changes manifested in the majority of children at a given age. In this sense, we are defining normal in a statistical, not an ethical, sense. This definition has considerable merit, as cultures that inhibit normal occurrences often do so at the risk of causing emotional disturbance in their members.

## Normal Developmental Stage

Following is a brief summary of each developmental stage, along with related psychosexual features and changes. Bear in mind that not all normal children proceed at the same rate or manner in development and that deviations do not necessarily indicate a serious problem.

### Infancy (Birth–1 Year)

In this stage, three phases of psychosexual development are common to both sexes. The first phase is called *pair-bonding*, or the oral stage of development. The infant derives great pleasure from sucking, body contact, cuddling, rocking movements, clinging, and touching. As the infant develops, these behaviors are expanded to include more transitional objects, such as soft blankets, furry stuffed animals, and favorite dolls. It is quite comforting for the infant to cling to a familiar blanket, to suck a thumb, and to rock rhythmically. By age two, the infant is responding to others by touching, kissing, and hugging. Infants also touch themselves in various ways, sometimes touching their genitals (unless punished for so doing). In normal development, genital touching is not a particular focus or intention during infancy; rather, infants seem to enjoy touching all parts of their body in random or quasi-intentional ways.

All of the above are vital for the infant's survival, as well as healthy emotional growth. For the infant to develop trust, it is important that the parent respond to these needs in a caring and thoughtful way. This ensures that the infant will feel safe and secure.

The second phase of psychosexual development in infancy is related to *genital play*. A male infant might have a penile erection at birth, and often will have an erection in the first few weeks of life, but this appears to be a reflexive rather than a sexual reaction. Although it is more difficult to prove, vaginal lubrication might occur in girls.

Both male and female infants respond to genital stimulation by becoming more relaxed and calmer.

Genital self-touching usually occurs between the ages of six and twelve months as part of a more general self-exploration of one's body. As infants become older, parents provide them with names for their genitals. This reduces the mystery surrounding such organs and promotes healthy psychosexual development.

Masturbation might occur during these first two years. It is evidenced by infants thrusting their pelvis when being cuddled or when falling asleep (with the aid of a blanket or doll). It usually begins during the following stage of development, when the child is three years old. It is important that parents do not punish the infant for self-stimulation or masturbation. Generally, such behaviors will diminish over time; paradoxically, punishment might cause masturbation to continue or even increase.

The third psychosexual phase is the child's identification of his or her *gender, or sex role* (occasionally not the same as his or her biological sex). The gender role of the infant determines how the parent will bring up the child, since standards of masculinity and femininity are still quite different. Having an assigned gender role helps the child to identify with the same sex parent and, more generally, with broader, socially approved sex role behaviors and standards.

### Toddler and Early Childhood (2–5 Years)

The toddler stage (2–3 years) in the development of sexuality is frequently termed the *anal stage*, as toddlers engage in major efforts to control bowel and bladder functions. Toilet training takes place primarily in this stage, sometimes with much pressure and anxiety attending such training. Common sexual behaviors observed in three-year-olds include handling of their own genitals, kissing parents and others, cuddling, and a beginning awareness of genital differences between males and females.

Following the toddler stage, children enter early childhood (4–5 years), characterized by the onset of the *phallic stage* of psychosexual

development. Directed genital play and specific sexual sensations and
feelings are first manifested at this stage. At age four, common sexual
behaviors include cuddling with family members, kissing, touching,
tickling, and mild masturbation. This marks the age when the child
shows increased curiosity about sex, asking questions such as "Where
do babies come from?" and "How do babies get out of their mothers?" This marks the stage when children purposely display their genitals to peers. They are often fascinated by excretion as well as sex,
being curious, giggly, and aroused by various bathroom matters. Alternatively, children at this stage are developing a need for increased
privacy, especially concerning excretion. Another characteristic behavior of this stage is the grasping of one's genitals and the associated
need to urinate when stressed or excited.

The five-year-old's behavior is quite different from that of the four-
year-old. Children at this age are more serious, self-contained, and
better able to imitate grown-up behavior. They understand that they
were in their mother's tummy before being born. Open genital display decreases, and children become more modest. Bathroom fascina-
tion also decreases. Children are aware of the physical differences between the sexes and usually wonder why males do not have breasts
and females do not have penises. They frequently play interpersonal
games, including family, marriage, doctor, and store. Boys and girls
play together, although the boys might reject female roles, tending to
imitate the adult male role; girls tend to play mainly female or dependent roles, especially that of mother or baby.

Throughout this stage, children are generally egocentric in their
thought patterns, looking primarily after their own gratification. Con-
science does begin to develop, however, along with an increased
ability to feel for others. Moreover, a degree of conventional moral
reasoning is evident by the end of this stage.

### Latency (6–9 Years)

The six-year-old has a greater awareness of and interest in the an-
atomical differences between the sexes. The child wants practical answers to questions about sex differences. Questions of how a baby

comes out of the mother's stomach and whether it hurts the mother in the process are quite common. The six-year-old often wants a new baby in the family, preferably of the same sex. Usually, if a baby is due, the six-year-old is extremely excited and yearns to hold and feed it. This is also the age of frequent giggling about words used to describe toileting functions, though on a more sophisticated level than that evident in the phallic stage. The six-year-old thinks in terms of marrying someone of the opposite sex. Doll play is elaborate for traditionally raised females, and domestic play for both sexes continues with family, school, and hospital or doctor, with boys taking on the male roles.

At the age of seven, the topic of birth is still in the forefront. The seven-year-old can associate a pregnant woman with a baby and usually asks questions about the details of birth. Children at this age are more discreet about their bodies, displaying more modesty about using the bathroom and anxiety about being touched. Children often talk about boyfriends and girlfriends, as well as joking about love and marriage (of each other). One of the favorite songs sung is this:

> *Johnny and Margie sitting in a tree,*
> *K-I-S-S-I-N-G.*
> *First comes love, then comes marriage,*
> *Then comes Annie in a baby carriage.*
> *Sucking her thumb,*
> *Wetting her pants,*
> *Doing a hoochy-koochy dance.*

Domestic play continues, with an increased use of costumes, especially for girls. Boys tend to enjoy building and playing in forts, tree houses, and tents. Occasional masturbation is common, but not all children engage in it. Intense or frequent masturbation tends to be more problematic and is often a sign of anxiety, distress, or sexual abuse.

As latency progresses (8–9 years), an increase in secretive behavior among peers is observed. Children need more privacy, exchange the latest dirty jokes, and gossip about relationships. There is an increase in hero worship, especially of athletes and movie, television, and rock stars. The child's room might be plastered with related posters interspersed with younger-age toys, pictures, stuffed animals, and dolls. Clothing becomes more important, as children become increasingly conscious of social fads and pressures. Peer groups and cliques start to emerge, with a general interest in socialization becoming much stronger. Specific sexual interest remains diffuse, and sexual behavior is absent or discreet. Little change in sexual organs or hormones takes place during this stage, thus giving it its name (latency).

### Preadolescence (10–12 Years)

At this stage of sexual development, initial signs of puberty emerge with the development of secondary sexual characteristics. The onset of puberty seems triggered by biochemical factors, which are related to some extent to general nutrition. This has been occurring at progressively younger ages over the course of this century.

In girls, the onset of puberty is usually marked by the appearance of breast buds, slight elevations of the breast and nipple. Pubic hair might precede breast budding in some girls, but it generally follows. In boys, changes usually occur six months to a year later than in girls. These changes are characterized by a growth in the testes and scrotum, accompanied by the thinning and reddening of the scrotal skin. At this time or shortly after, pubic hairs start to appear. The boy might experience enlargement of his breasts, but this usually regresses after a year.

Marked changes in height and weight during preadolescence is generally limited to girls. Boys are generally one to two years behind girls throughout puberty. Consequently, most of the girls tower over the boys, a cause of concern for late-maturing boys and the reason why many girls are attracted to older boys who are physically (and psychologically) more compatible. Strong friendships develop during this stage, frequently consisting of feelings of strong affection and loyalty. Children often choose a same sex best friend with whom they share their deepest feelings. Budding romances also occur, with boys acting as quite the gentlemen to their ladies. For instance, a boy might carry a girl's books and protect her from the teasing and torments of others. Preadolescent girls without boyfriends tend to tease or snicker about these relationships, but they are usually quite jealous.

One of the games boys and girls play during this stage is called "slap and tickle." In this game, boys and girls hit one another or tickle one another in a playful manner acceptable to both sexes. Some degree of sexuality might be present, but it does not seem directly motivated by sexual concerns.

### Early Adolescence (13–15 Years)

Two major changes occur during this stage: pubertal maturation and intense interest in (and pressure from) peer group involvement. Entrance into high school, with its associated adjustments, is another transition. All these changes are stressful to the adolescent's environment, personality, and psychosexuality.

In girls, the landmark event indicating pubertal maturation is menstruation. Menstruation occurs when the inside lining of the womb thickens to produce a place where a fertilized egg (ovum) could develop. If the egg is not fertilized, the extra lining is shed, which produces the menstrual period. Girls are often frightened after the onset of their first period because they do not expect it or have limited knowledge about this physiological process; they often worry that something is drastically wrong. Even if knowledgeable, they are often repulsed or disgusted by the bloody discharge. Other bodily changes occur as well, as is shown in table 2–1.

In boys, the landmark event signaling pubertal maturation is ejaculation, an event occurring after the penis becomes erect and aroused in some manner, either during a dream or through fondling. The resulting sensation becomes increasingly pleasurable, leading to an orgasm, or climax, wherein ejaculation of sperm (within seminal fluid) takes place. Boys are rarely frightened by their first ejaculation because it feels so good, although many misinterpret it as urinary excretion of some sort. Table 2–1 summarizes other changes boys experience during puberty.

In both males and females, this stage produces strong sexual feel-

## Table 2–1
## CHANGES IN PUBERTY

| *Females* | *Males* |
|---|---|
| Face becomes fuller | Facial hair appears |
| Acne possibly appears | Acne possibly appears |
| Voice deepens slightly | Voice breaks and deepens |
| Upper arms become fatter | Shoulders broaden |
| Underarm hair appears | Underarm hair appears |
| Nipples stand out | Arms become thicker and more muscular |
| Breasts enlarge | Penis grows darker and bigger |
| Pubic hair continues to grow | Pubic hair appears and grows |
| Genitals become fleshier and darken | Testicles enlarge |
| Skin becomes oilier and coarser | Skin becomes oilier and coarser |
| Height and weight increase | Height and weight increase |
| Female figure emerges | Muscle mass increases |
| Sweating increases | Sweating increases |
| Hair on arms and legs grows | Hair on arms and legs grows |
| Buttocks become fattier | Hair grows on chest and back |
| Hips and thighs become fattier | Legs become more muscular |

ings. Sexual dreams and fantasies are typical and plentiful, as is interest in reading about and viewing romantic, sensual, and erotic stories. It is at this stage that adult movies and reading material become the object of keen interest. Self-stimulation and genital masturbation frequently occur. Heterosexual behavior such as dating, kissing, and petting often take place. Adolescents experience a strong appeal of love and romance, along with intense pressure to enter romantic heterosexual relationships. Going out with someone becomes a mark of status and acceptance in the peer group society (especially for girls). Adolescents become greatly distressed if they are not accepted by their peers, sometimes going to great lengths to obtain such acceptance, often to the point of violating major family, school, and moral rules.

Presumably, homosexual (or bisexual) feelings also are evident at this stage, but they tend to be strongly repressed, owing to the harsh treatment such behavior receives among adolescents. Being labeled a "queer" or a "fag" is considered the worst fate possible. It is not until much latter that genuinely homosexual youths feel that they can come out of the closet.

### Adolescence (16–20 Years)

This stage of sexual development is viewed as a period of change, friction, and problems. Adolescent boys and girls begin assuming adult roles. They are encouraged to be more independent and assertive but often are frustrated by cultural, financial, legal, and educational restrictions. In the sexual arena, physiological sexuality is at its height precisely when open sexuality is sharply criticized by parents, teachers, and society in general. This causes major internal and external conflicts to arise as adolescents experience confusing and mixed feelings: their bodies are saying one thing, and their minds, morals, and parents are saying something else. The resulting conflicts over independence, separation, and sexuality are often so overwhelming that adolescents often act out their frustration by using sexual relationships to gain distance from family problems and achieve some measure of acceptance and release of tension. Hence, adolescents frequently violate sexual restrictions at least to some extent.

Without adequate information regarding sexual activity, adolescents often suffer serious consequences of unchecked sexuality, such as out-of-wedlock pregnancies, abortions, or venereal disease. Fortunately, most adolescents use their growing intellectual skills and their respect for rules in general to avoid these pitfalls and develop a strong and stable sense of identity with equally strong feelings of self-worth.

Adolescents continue the early adolescent zeal of needing companionship and wanting a personal relationship, but they appear more comfortable being alone or otherwise independent from the group. For many adolescents, the focus turns increasingly to career plans and goals, as the needs for career definition and intimacy become more balanced (unlike the dominance of relationship needs in the previous stage). This prepares late adolescents for the impending crises of adulthood and the delicate integration of primary needs.

## Stage-Specific Effects
## of Sexual Abuse

For children to enter adulthood with a sense of self-worth and a secure self-image, it is crucial that they be successful in completing prior developmental stages. Sexual abuse frequently interferes with the normal progression of these stages, causing changes in the rate of progression through the stages (pseudomature or delayed development), as well as stage-specific problems depending on the point(s) at which the abuse occurs.

Sexual abuse is extremely traumatic, often overwhelming a child's limited defenses and coping mechanisms. The child's mind cannot understand or accept what is happening, so the mind and body split during the incident. The mind pretends that the abuse is not scary, allowing for some degree of personal control. The child often thinks that he or she has provoked the abuse, which makes the child feel guilty and responsible. In turn, the child believes that he or she is in control rather than powerless and out of control. As long as the child remains in control, he or she thinks that everything is all right. This strategy places the burden of the abuse on the victim rather than the abuser. This allows the child to cope with the trauma to some extent, but it frequently hinders developmental growth. The ongoing tension usually erupts into emotional and behavioral problems intrinsically related to the stage during which the abuse occurred. Following are some common examples of such problems:

### Infancy (Birth–1 Year)

Displacing of fear and anxiety through excessive crying and fretful behavior

Physical ailments such as vomiting, feeding problems, bowel disturbances, and sleep problems

Failure to thrive

### *Toddler and Early Childhood (2–5 Years)*

Fear of a particular person or place

Regression to earlier forms of behavior such as bed-wetting, stranger anxiety, separation anxiety, thumb sucking, baby talk, whining, and clinging

Victimization of others

Fear of being abandoned if the caretaker cannot come to the child's assistance or momentarily leaves

Feelings of strong shame or guilt

Excessive masturbation

### *Latency (6–9 Years)*

Nightmares and other sleep disturbances

Fear that the attack will recur

Phobias concerning specific school or community activities or specific people

Withdrawal from family and friends

Regression to earlier behaviors

Eating disturbances

Physical ailments such as abdominal pain or urinary difficulties

### *Preadolescence (10–12 Years)*

Depression

Nightmares and other sleep disturbances

Poor school performance

Promiscuity

Use of illegal drugs or alcohol

Fear that the attack will recur

Eating disturbances

Regression to earlier behaviors

Withdrawal from family and friends

Aggression

*Early Adolescence and Adolescence (13–20 Years)*

Running away from home

Severe depression

Early marriage

Promiscuity (sometimes to the point of prostitution)

Early pregnancy

Use of illegal drugs or alcohol

Suicidal thoughts or gestures

School truancy

Poor school performance

Pronounced fear that the attack will recur

Grief over the loss of one's virginity

Anger and rage about being forced into a situation beyond one's control

Difficulty in forming positive nonabusive relationships with the opposite sex

Withdrawal from family and friends

Pseudomature behaviors

Although the behavioral characteristics listed above are categorized under specific developmental stages, they might appear at somewhat earlier or later stages depending on the specific child, family, context in which the abuse occurred, and availability of support structures. Certain general problems, such as regression, anxiety, inappropriate sexual behavior, and behavioral difficulties, occur throughout the stages, varying mainly in the particular form or content of the expression.

# 3

# Abusive Encounters

SEXUAL abuse of children can occur in many ways and in many contexts. It can happen in the neighborhood, school, playground, or family. It can involve an adult, an adolescent, or another child. The victim and the offender may be male or female. Despite this diversity, one fact seems paramount: In most cases, the abuse of a child is perpetrated by a person familiar to the child; the anonymous child molester is extremely uncommon. It is estimated that more than 90 percent of child sexual abuse cases involve a person whom the child knows well, often one with whom the child has a strong bond (Russell 1986).

From data reported thus far, the majority of offenders (around 80 percent) are male, and the majority of victims (about 70 percent) are female (Finkelhor 1984). Recent reports suggest a somewhat more equalizing trend, however, particularly in the case of victims. It appears that sexual abuse of boys is considerably more prevalent than was previously believed and that women perpetrators are not as uncommon as was previously thought. In both matters, perhaps because of subtle and complex resistances in communication and different sex role expectations, boys are less likely to report the abuse or to be suspected of being abused, whereas women are less likely to be suspected of being perpetrators of abuse. In any case, the adult male–female child scenario is still the most common, a pattern congruent with the larger pattern of cultural sex role differences concerning dating, courtship, sex initiative, seduction, rape, and other sexually related areas. To the extent that sexual abuse is an expression of power as well as sexuality, the preponderance of male offenders again fits the larger cultural sex role of males displaying far more problems involving power and aggression.

## Contexts

Although there are many contexts in which sexual abuse could occur, it might be helpful to consider the following three general ones.

### Family (Incest)

Ranking first in prevalence and power, sexual abuse occurring in the family, or incest, is particularly harmful to the child because it produces a marked warping in family functioning and boundaries. In the most common type, that between father and daughter, incest causes the daughter to be elevated to a pseudoadult position, while the mother is demoted to an outsider position. Typically, the father and daughter form a strong bond based on a form of manipulation, while the mother remains either ignorant or knowledgeable but helplessly passive. The family realigns itself in this deviant way, with the daughter becoming the more favored and powerful "executive child," who adopts many adult roles and behaviors. Under the surface, however, she is usually extremely confused, ambivalent, and angry. This anger is often repressed, although it occasionally surfaces in intense rage at both father and mother—father for abusing her and mother for not protecting her. Together with this rage is a pervasive feeling of sadness and abandonment, as the child feels deeply alone, manipulated, abused, and unsupported. Such a child might appear to be powerful and well liked, sometimes even a princess in the house, but underneath she is deeply disturbed. Mother-son incest is much less common, but the dynamics of this type of incest are considered to be similar to those of father-daughter incest.

Sibling incest is probably the most underreported of all abusive encounters because it often borders on normal sexual play and experimentation and reporting is inhibited by strong bonds of alliance and resistance to squealing. Studies of such encounters typically show a gradual pattern of touching and sexual play leading to sexual abuse that is difficult to gauge, unless it becomes overtly violent. Children want to fit in with and be accepted by their peers. This is especially so with older siblings and the friends of these siblings. A younger child will do much (and purposely not tell) to gain an older sibling's affection and acceptance. When couched in a secret ritual and adult-like behavior, the temptations and pressures are almost irresistible for younger children.

A third area of sexual abuse occurring in a family is that between a relative (such as an uncle, aunt, grandfather, grandmother, or cousin) and a child. This is quite common but is usually more easily detected and somewhat less complicated for the child. Once again, an adult betrays the child's trust and affection in a flagrantly manipulative way.

Another area of family abuse lies in the murky but increasingly frequent interrelationships stemming from divorce and remarriage. Newly constituted families do not have the same shared history or bonds (biological and environmental) as natural families. As such, there is usually more limit-testing behavior and relatively free expression of feelings and impulses, sometimes leading to physically or sexually abusive behavior. Conversely, in cases where parents prolong custody battles, using the children as weapons to attack each other, allegations of sexual abuse by one of the parents is not uncommon. It is interesting that in such cases, unlike any other area, children have been noted to lie about sexual abuse. Frequency of abuse within and among all the possible coalitions of children and stepparents, stepsiblings, steprelatives (outside the nuclear family), halfsiblings, adoptive siblings, and so on is unknown but suspected to be quite high.

### Family, Friends, Acquaintances and Surrogate Authority Figures

A second sphere of sexual abuse arises in contact the child might have with a neighbor, friend of the family, local person who enjoys being with children, teacher, baby-sitter, housekeeper, gardener, and so on. These people typically have a relationship with the family as a whole. They often play certain roles or execute certain functions that are helpful for the family as a group or for the child in particular. The child typically enters a relationship with such a person in a task-oriented or otherwise pleasurable way, all the while being subtly manipulated and seduced. Physical force is rare in these situations, as children are coaxed to enter into "special" games and activities, which they are urged to keep strictly secret.

In the case of authority figures (such as baby-sitters or teachers), aspects of obedience, submission, and even duty are present, as well as bonds of affection. Such a mixture becomes extremely confusing to the child, who wants to obey and please. Such scenarios continue into adulthood in the working world, where countless employees are subject to sexual coercion by employers or supervisors.

## Strangers

Sexual abuse of a child by a total stranger (or even a remote acquaintance) is a rare happening, just as rape of an adult by a total stranger is rare. It does occur at times, however, chiefly in the context of significant force, bribery, or manipulation. Even in these cases, violence is rare, although an actual or perceived threat of violence is always present. The child in these situations feels threatened and in danger. Because of these distinctly negative feelings, with no counteracting positive bonds or obligations in regard to the perpetrator, the child is most likely to reveal the incident or demonstrate behavior that is highly revealing itself. Unless the perpetrator has made a direct, concrete, and aggressive threat, which the child believes to be realistic, abuse by a stranger is likely to be reported or detected. Even in cases of maximum force, the child will almost always display marked symptoms outside his or her verbal behavior. Because of the likelihood that these cases will be reported, and because they are in many ways easier to deal with (lacking the complexity and mixed feelings present in cases where the perpetrator is a familiar and positive figure), they often have a far better outcome in the long run.

## Factors Affecting Severity

Although sexual abuse of children causes significant emotional damage in terms of both short-term and long-term consequences, several factors alter the magnitude of such damage. A child forced to engage in painful anal intercourse with a person whom he disdains, while being physically abused and harshly threatened, will be much more affected than a child who is fondled in a somewhat gentle way by a well-liked neighbor. Several factors work together to produce different degrees of emotional distress. Among the most prominent factors are the following.

### Frequency and Duration

Episodes of abuse that occur more frequently and for a longer period of time produce greater distress than isolated or infrequent incidents, given the relative equality of other variables. Isolated incidents of sexual abuse (or at least unwanted sexual advances) have probably been perpetrated against most people in the United States. Throughout the ages, women in particular have been exposed to such sexual advances or abuse by men. Sexual abuse that occurs over a long period of time tends to become implanted in one's personality and mode of interacting with other people.

### Type of Encounter

The exact nature of the sexual abuse, both in terms of context and specific details, is another important variable affecting the severity of the outcome. Whether or not physical force and aggression were involved is particularly important, as these often cause acute fear and revulsion and are associated with more traumatic outcomes. Whether or not the sexual actions caused physical pain is another variable. Hence, encounters involving penetration, anal sex, oral sex (especially causing choking or gagging), or sadistic behavior of any kind are construed by the child in a much more negative light than episodes involving cuddling, petting, fondling, touching, or looking.

### Relationship between Child and Perpetrator

The precise nature of the relationship between the child and the perpetrator is extremely important in ascertaining the meaning and significance of sexual abuse. However, no simple formula exists for relating the severity of the encounter to the intensity of the relationship. Although close relationships generally offer much more familiarity and possibility for intimacy, especially compared with encounters with strangers or acquaintances, such relationships are generally much more volatile and ambivalent. Hence, an encounter with a relative stranger, although distinctly negative, might be far simpler to handle and work through than the complex and ambivalent relationship a child would have with a familiar person. In any case, the nature of the relationship affects the meaning of the sexual interaction, typically causing it to have different connotations and consequences. Some of these connotations and consequences might be favorable, such as when a child achieves more attention or power as the result of engaging in a sexual encounter. Similarly, a child who is feeling lonely or rejected might gain some much-needed solace and support by an apparently warm encounter with a person who seems to care for him or her.

### Child Characteristics

Characteristics of a given child strongly influence the amount of emotional harm that he or she is likely to suffer from sexual abuse. Such characteristics include chronological age, developmental level, intelligence, social perceptiveness, sensitivity to criticism, need for affiliation, and level of self-esteem. These individual characteristics affect the degree of emotional distress experienced by the child. Generally, the younger, less intelligent, less sensitive, and less needy a child, the less likely it is that he or she will experience acute emotional distress; the older, more intelligent, more sensitive, and more dependent the child, the more likely it is that he or she will be profoundly affected by the abuse.

### Sex Characteristics

Whether the abuser and the abused are of the same sex or opposite sexes seems to be very important in affecting the meaning of the sex-

ual abuse. Same sex offenders of children violate two taboos at once—
the coercion of a minor into sexual activity and the forced participation in homosexual activities. Since the general culture is generally
disdainful of (or has a hard time accepting) homosexual relations of
any kind, it views homosexual encounters, especially those involving
children, as distinctly more negative than heterosexual encounters.
This feeling filters down from the adult culture into the lives of children, routinely exemplified in the antagonism children express when
they refer to a peer as being a "queer," "fag," or "sissy." Similarly,
because of the double taboo that is broken, victims of homosexual
child abuse appear to be more reluctant to disclose the nature and
details of such encounters, fearing more criticism and experiencing
more anxiety and embarrassment. Heterosexual encounters, although
violating the adult-child boundary, are in accord with prevailing heterosexual values and have even been popularized in many works of
acknowledged and appreciated fantasy (*Lolita,*a novel by Vladimir
Nabokov, is an excellent example).

### Social Repercussions

Whether other people or circumstances are affected by the sexual
abuse is another important variable affecting severity. Sexual abuse
that is conducted publicly or made public knowledge is much more
detrimental (at least in the short term) to a child's well-being than
more discreet actions performed privately. In the former instance, the
child is forced to deal with other people who might know of the
abuse and who could (and often do) use the abuse as a means of
manipulation or control. In addition, a child whose sexual abuse is
made public is exposed to much more criticism and teasing, leading
to heightened anxiety and embarrassment.

## Ploys

Sexual abuse situations are quite dissimilar, varying in countless ways.
They are characterized by different ploys perpetrators use to attempt
to give the abuse some meaning and value so as to prevent disclosure

by the child. Typically, perpetrators use one of the following five ploys, although occasionally they combine ploys, particularly in the beginning or ending stages.

The most prevalent and, arguably, the most pernicious of these ploys is that of couching the sexual abuse in terms of *love and affection*. The perpetrator provides nurturance, often to a child in dire need of it, in return for increasing physical favors of a sexual nature. Silence is requested because of the unique and "special" quality of the interaction, as the child is told that other people would not understand their special relationship. Rarely is this relationship truly mutual or caring, however, as the child is merely an instrument to give the perpetrator pleasure. Since this type of approach mirrors the fusion of love and sex prevalent in the adult culture, the child does not perceive it as being particularly abnormal, at least at first. What makes it more problematic and detrimental is the dramatic age difference of the parties involved. This kind of situation is very disturbing to a child because it sends two conflicting messages: (1) Sexual play is an expression of love and (2) sexual play is taboo (not to be told to others because they would find it bad). Eventually, the child loses a sense of trust, particularly if the adult is in (or close to) the family. Love is no longer unconditional or a source of fundamental acceptance.

A second ploy couches the sexual abuse in a pretense of affection, while instilling in the child an overwhelming sense of *guilt* if he or she reveals the truth. The perpetrator makes statements such as the following: "You don't want Uncle Ben to go to jail, do you? That's what they'll do to me if you tell them. I'll be thrown in a dreary, dark, cold dungeon with rats and roaches, and I'll be all alone." The child is induced to feel guilty about telling, while characteristically feeling even more guilty about the sexual interaction itself. Guilt causes anxiety and withdrawal as the child becomes increasingly worried, passive, and self-conscious. Even after disclosure, guilt continues to operate, as the accusatory nature of the legal sysem, coupled with the usual plight of the perpetrator, tend to fulfill (at least to a point) the predictions of gloom. The child then feels to blame for what happened to the perpetrator, and sometimes for the very sexual actions.

A third ploy perpetrators use, especially when the intrinsic bond is weaker and there is less time spent in seduction, is that of *bribery*. Children are promised (or given) material goods or are allowed to engage in certain highly pleasurable activities as direct rewards for permitting sexual play. The archetypal image of a dirty old man offering candy if a child will pull down his or her pants (or touch the man's penis) is a case in point. Despite its flagrantly manipulative quality, this scenario is somewhat easier for the child to handle and understand, as the child receives a reward for an activity that is mutually assumed to be wrong (or at best neutral). This is in stark contrast to the first two ploys, which try to convince the child of the virtues of the sexual encounter. The child is still faced with an acute dilemma, however: whether to gain a good end through bad means.

Verbal *threats* of many kinds constitute a fourth ploy. The perpetrator often predicts dire consequences and makes up elaborate stories of what will happen (and has happened to others) if the child tells. Threats include direct physical violence to the child, disclosure to the child's friends, aggression toward loved objects (friends, relatives, pets, toys, and so on), or destruction of property. Threats increase anxiety through fear of negative consequences, and the child becomes immobilized as a result, blindly and passively accepting the abuse as the lesser of two evils.

A final ploy consists of the use of actual *force*, chiefly of a direct, physical nature. This is most frequently encountered in episodes of a one-time nature, particularly with strangers. This ploy basically amounts to rape, as defined by the fusion of sex and aggression, wherein one party aggressively forces sex onto an unwilling partner. Obviously, this scenario causes acute and intense fear, but at least the child usually has few reservations about telling because he or she believes that the worst has already occurred. Threats of murder or other severe consequences might counteract this one positive effect. Other factors being equal, sexual abuse of a forceful nature is considered to be the most traumatic type of abuse.

# 4

# Effects of Sexual Abuse: Short Term and Long Term

H OW can one tell whether a child has been sexually abused? What are the immediate effects of sexual abuse? What happens over time in sexual abuse cases; do children ever get over the fact of being sexually abused? Parents and teachers commonly ask these and other questions concerning victims of sexual abuse. Unfortunately, not much is known about the precise effects of such encounters, in part because sexual abuse cases have only recently begun to be studied in a systematic way and in part because of the incredible variety and complexity of the cases themselves. Cases that involve a great deal of fear, intensity, pain, or aggression are much more immediately traumatic than cases in which sexual interactions take place in a more gentle and caring manner. Moreover, cases that have continued over a long period of time in a relatively frequent manner seem to have more powerful effects than cases in which abuse has happened once or a few times. Despite these and other significant differences among various sexual abuse cases, parents can observe some common effects that indicate possible sexual abuse.

## Impact of Sexual Abuse

Sexual abuse is unique as an offense, differing from other forms of abuse in that it affects many areas of functioning. David Finkelhor of the Family Violence Research Program at the University of New

Hampshire has identified four core injuries caused by child sexual abuse (Finkelhor 1984):

Traumatic sexualization

Betrayal

Stigmatization

Powerlessness

Child victims of such assaults are prematurely exposed, in highly traumatic ways, to the complexities of sexual experience, often with disastrous consequences. They also feel betrayed by, and often lose trust in, adults; this is particularly so when a formerly trustworthy or seemingly caring adult has abused them. Child victims feel embarrassed, humiliated, and stigmatized by the experience and are often deeply ashamed and plagued by guilt. Lastly, victims experience an overwhelming sense of powerlessness, feeling as though they have little control over their lives and relationships.

Although this framework supplies a very useful way of explaining the unique trauma engendered by abuse, the presenting features are somewhat different, causing direct and concrete changes in behavior and mood. Before looking at these changes in more detail, it is important to recognize that the specific impact of a particular sexual abuse case can be substantially modified by the following factors, which can serve to mediate the direct effects of abuse:

Chronological age (the psychic trauma is generally greater with younger children)

Developmental level(s) of the child (cognitively and psychosexually)

Child's emotional health prior to the abuse

Frequency of abuse

Nature of the abuse (whether it entailed intensity, force, trauma, and so on)

How the child perceived the action

Nature of the nonsexual relationship between the child and the offender and the child's associated feelings

Supportiveness of family, school, peer, and community groups

Strength of the family system

Availability of supportive figures and helping professionals

These factors modify the impact of abuse in either direction, making it more or less traumatic.

## Presenting Features

Although many problems can and do occur as a result of sexual abuse, the following four general changes are the most common and important:

*Alteration in the child's feelings, awareness, and behavior in reference to sexuality.* This change appears to be at the core of the child's problem, as the child becomes overly knowledgeable and acts deviantly in regard to sexual concerns. The child typically will have strong reactions to physical contact and displays of affection, particularly if they include any hint of sexual contact. For instance, a child might stiffen when touched on the leg, resist being hugged, flinch, or even scream in fear when inadvertently touched in the genital or anal region.

Children who have been sexually abused display greatly heightened sexual awareness and sophistication, along with age-inappropriate knowledge regarding sexuality. They frequently know several names (including slang and swear words) for sexual organs and seem to comprehend the nature and process of specific sexual acts at a level far beyond that typically displayed by peers. Conversely, abused children sometimes show excessive ignorance of such matters, staunchly denying any knowledge whatsoever but exhibiting acute distress, agitation, and defensiveness during the questioning.

Deviant sexual behavior is yet another characteristic, as demonstrated by either extreme fear, sensitivity, and withdrawal from physical contact on the one hand or excessive sexual play on the other. Such children often engage in compulsive sexual play with other children, tending to repeat the scene in which the abuse occurred. They tend to engage in fantasies about sex, frequently depicting such fantasies in stories, drawings, constructions, and play. Another common manifestation is one of incessant and agitated masturbation, often to the point of causing soreness and discoloration (usually redness). Adolescents who have been abused often become overly seductive, promiscuous, and apt to engage in more extreme forms of sexual acting out, such as prostitution, participation in more unusual sexual practices, repeated victimization of an almost masochistic nature, or repeated seduction or abuse of others.

*Regression in physiological and behavioral functioning.* A second main feature observed in sexually abused children is a fairly abrupt and significant negative change in sleeping, eating, independent activity, stability, consistency, school performance, bowel and bladder control, and social relationships. Children characteristically act the way they did when younger, displaying regression in one or more of the above areas. A common example is the sudden onset of a multitude of fears and associated coping mechanisms, which the child ostensibly outgrew at an earlier age. Thus, it is not unusual to see such children sleeping once again with a teddy bear, carrying around a special blanket, being afraid of the dark or loud noises, wetting the bed, and so on.

*Interpersonal problems.* School performance is similarly affected, as overt behavior and task performance both become more problematic. Children are often considered to be agitated and "immature," as well as failing to accomplish tasks and complete assigned work.

Socially, sexually abused children typically become more withdrawn and agitated. Such children tend to display greater isolation from peers and increased separation anxiety when apart from nonoffending parents. Occasionally, children become rashly pseudoindependent and overtly rebellious of authority. At such times, they become interested in concerns typically associated with older children (sex being a prime example) and demand more adultlike privileges. Children often engage in these behaviors in compulsive and angry ways, sometimes to the point of overt aggression and other antisocial behaviors.

*Emotional distress.* Sexually abused children are more worried, fearful, sensitive, nervous, irritable, moody, angry, depressed, and unstable than are their counterparts who have not been abused. Another set of symptoms frequently expressed revolve around assorted physical complaints or problems, often of a psychosomatic nature. These include bed-wetting (enuresis) and bed-soiling (encopresis), headaches, stomachaches, nervous twitching, excessive blinking, and preoccupation with bodily ailments (hypochondriasis). These symptoms are more frequently observed in younger children than in adolescents.

Although children demonstrate agitation and anxiety in all spheres, it is most evident in the context(s) in which the abuse occurred, particularly in reference to the specific perpetrator and the actual place(s) where the abuse occurred. Children display the most agitation toward the perpetrator, becoming emotionally aroused in interaction with him or her and often becoming highly ambivalent about this person's merits.

Although the prevailing emotion exhibited by sexually abused children is heightened anxiety, other forms of emotional distress also are apparent. This distress usually takes one of two forms, depression or anger. Parallel to the twin regression routes, depression and anger are linked to their behavioral stances of extreme dependence and extreme independence, respectively.

More girls adopt the depressive position and more boys the anger position. The reasons for this are not clear, but it is congruent with the prevailing social stereotypes, the different manner in which boys and girls are raised, and possibly differing social-emotional processing abilities between the sexes. Boys tend to display more anger and related behavioral problems of an acting-out or externalizing nature but rarely if ever reveal or discuss the abusive situations that preceded their problematic behaviors. In fact, boys work hard at repressing the trauma, often forgetting what happened and otherwise avoiding the memories at any cost. Girls tend to dwell on the memories and are often overcome with feelings of helplessness, fear, sadness, humiliation, embarrassment, and guilt. This causes them to withdraw from social contact and to avoid emotional encounters that generate arousal, particularly those that have any trace of anger. Instead, they internalize stress to a great extent and thus have problems resolving their complex and ambivalent feelings, particularly those involving anger. Just as boys have a hard time expressing sadness and vulnerability, girls have a hard time expressing anger. These are generalizations, as some boys become very depressed and some girls very angry. Nonetheless, these two routes tend to hold for boys and girls most of the time, especially in preschoolers and elementary school children.

Sex differences in adolescent behaviors are not as marked, as girls display much more direct anger; boys, however, display no more (and usually even less) overt depression. In general, adolescents tend to become pseudoindependent and display a great deal of anger, cynicism, and rage. In addition to heightened sexual behavior, they are likely to get into frequent clashes with authority, to do poorly in school, and to engage in antisocial activities (such as stealing, aggression, and running away).

## Short-Term and Long-Term Effects

### Short-Term Effects

Specific short-term effects are typically manifestations of the above three major changes. Short-term effects usually appear immediately after the onset of sexual abuse and linger until the abuse is recognized, expressed, or somehow worked through by the child. Although no two cases are exactly the same, many of the following behavioral indicators are present in children who have been sexually abused. Since many of these behaviors exist within broad samples of average children, it is most significant if the child has changed with respect to the following characteristics, especially if such changes occur suddenly:

Extreme withdrawal or passivity

Social isolation in school, on the playground, or in the neighborhood

Fearfulness and anxiety

Depression

Insecurity when alone or when in the presence of certain adults and sometimes adults in general

Decreased attention span, together with increase in daydreaming

Oversensitivity and reactivity

Displays of temperament, particularly aggression and violence, when provoked

Chronic lethargy and feelings of being tired, often exemplified by dozing or sleeping during class

Nightmares, particularly of people attacking, abusing, or assaulting them

Physical signs of change, including injury, irritation, pain, bleeding, swelling, or discharge within the genital or anal areas

Changes in attitude or behavior regarding sexuality

Sexual talk or knowledge beyond the child's mental or social age

Regressive behaviors such as crying excessively, bed-wetting, over-dependence, thumb sucking, nail biting, and sleeping with stuffed animals

Sudden and evident strain in the child's relationship with another person that is not easily explicable or understood

Heightened immaturity

Attempts at isolation or escape, by constantly seeking privacy or running away

Psychosomatic symptoms, particularly ailments or pains that seem to have no medical cause

Direct or indirect hints that something of a sinister nature might be happening

General irritability without clear cause

Once again, the presence of one or even a few of these signs is not necessarily indicative of sexual abuse. When many of these are present or a few of these are present in very intense and changed ways, the possibility of sexual abuse must be more actively explored, preferably by talking to the child in a direct, caring way. Since many of these signs are indicators of overall general stress, sexual abuse will not always be found, especially if the child has only a few of the symptoms. Regardless of the reasons for these behavioral changes, however, it is wise for any parent or teacher to find out the cause of them and to work on whatever underlying stress there might be.

### Long-Term Effects

Long-term effects of sexual abuse are much less clear, mainly because few controlled studies of long-term outcomes have been conducted. (For reviews of studies, see Finkelhor 1984; Russell 1986.) What is known represents a smattering of clinical case history knowledge, retrospective accounts by adults who have been abused, and a few outcome studies of treated cases. In general, the therapeutic resolution of sexual abuse at a young age appears to be healthy, as fewer long-term effects are observed in adults who were treated while children or adolescents. Untreated cases appear to have many long-term effects, often of a much more problematic nature. These effects, for both treated and untreated cases (with the former showing less intensity, frequency, and severity), include the following:

Problems in establishing and maintaining heterosexual relationships

Sexual problems, often pertaining to achieving sexual satisfaction for oneself or others

Low sexual self-esteem, a measure of how an adult views his or her sexual identity and related strengths, interests, attractiveness, and abilities

Lower self-esteem in general

Unwilled memories or nightmares of the sexual abuse incidents (flashbacks)

General problems sustaining relationships and jobs

Anxiety, fearfulness, and insecurity

Social passivity and withdrawal

Melancholy and depression, sometimes reaching suicidal proportions

Suspiciousness, sometimes verging on paranoia

Increased homosexual behavior (about four times normal rates) in men who were abused as children by older males

Increased negative feelings about the perpetrator and other members of his or her sex

Overall depressive effect on socioeconomic class

*Perhaps the most sinister long-term effect consists of the fact that boy victims are far more apt to become future sexual offenders and girl victims to become further exploited or victimized.*

These long-term effects are not of a precise or direct nature, and as such cannot be seen as specific signs or symptoms. What is important to recognize is that sexual abuse, particularly when untreated, often has major ramifications in many areas of functioning and rarely disappears with age. Although people can repress the actual abuse episodes, the abuse continues to have an effect on a more subconscious (and thus pernicious) level. In this regard, the abuse affects characteristics such as general mood, relationships with other people, job stability, and various aspects of personality. The dirty secret continues to fester.

## Aftermath of Abuse

The feelings people experience in the wake of abuse follow quite a predictable pattern. An immediate traumatic reaction is typically observed, causing a great deal of anxiety and fear, which are often accompanied by feelings of disgust, shame, and (slight) depression. These feelings are quickly transformed into anger and rage, which help the victim regain a semblance or normalcy and achieve greater independence and self-confidence. Moreover, the family and social network typically provide a great deal of consistent, positive support.

In incest cases, matters are much more complicated because the feelings generated in the various family members are extremely strong, unstable, inconsistent, and ambivalent. The stages through which the victim achieves resolution are considerably different from those experienced by the offender or other family members. There are, however, fairly predictable patterns of progression for each family member, as is shown in table 4–1.

As this table indicates, many of the feeling states experienced by different family members are similar in nature but dissimilar in the time at which they appear. Hence, nonoffending spouses are quick to experience and demonstrate anger, especially toward the offender, but slow to feel the deeper depression that they inevitably experience. Likewise, victims typically feel very guilty soon after the abuse has been disclosed, particularly if they told someone about it, but offenders experience true guilt only after considerable time and treatment, if ever.

Table 4–1

STAGES OF SEXUAL ABUSE RESOLUTION IN INCEST CASES

| Victim | Sibling | Offender | Spouse |
|---|---|---|---|
| Anxiety | Surprise | Denial | Shock |
| Guilt, embarrassment | Anxiety | Anxiety, shame | Anger |
| Depression | Embarrassment | Depression | Depression |
| Anger | Resolution | Guilt | Resolution |
| Resolution | | Resolution | |

Parents and teachers must be aware of these stages, recognize that they are both normal and healthy, and realize that associated behaviors do not necessarily indicate that the child is struggling with a major problem. Rather, the focus should be on helping the victim work through each stage by listening, caring, and sympathizing, as well as by suggesting actions that will facilitiate better expression and understanding. A similar support process is equally important for other family members, since they also need considerable care and reassurance in coming to terms with the abuse.

# 5

# Whom Do I Believe?

A YOUNG girl tells you that she has been sexually abused by her uncle. How can you be sure she's telling the truth? Particularly because the allegation carries so much weight and could have a powerful effect on people's lives, it is important for you to be somewhat convinced that the child is telling the truth before taking steps. Even in cases of reasonable doubt, however, it is advisable to discuss the matter with other adults who have knowledge of the child and to consult someone who is more experienced in dealing with matters of sexual abuse.

## Assessing the Child's Credibility

The most important principle to remember is that *children rarely lie about sexual abuse.* Much more often, they are afraid to tell or, when they do tell, tend to downplay the actual episodes. There are, however, documented cases in which children have distorted the truth in some fashion, sometimes exaggerating details or making up stories that indirectly express their anger or provide satisfaction to a third party. In particular, children have been known to falsely accuse a parent of sexual abuse in heated divorce or custody cases; at such times, the child's accusation provides strong ammunition for the non-offending parent and thereby is tacitly reinforced in a powerful way. Aside from these cases, which are extremely rare, it is safe to assume that most children do not lie about sexual abuse. In exact testimony regarding details, however, children (similar to adults) display marked variations in memory. In general, younger children provide less complete and detailed testimony than older children.

It is wise to accept everything the child says as true, at least during the initial conversation, especially if he or she is concurrently demonstrating the primary features of inappropriate sexual knowledge or behavior, regression in one or more areas of functioning, and general anxiety and moodiness. After the conversation, assess the child's statements by checking out specifics (when possible) and by talking to her or him again on a different occasion to check consistency. Remember that a child's understanding of sexual actions might be somewhat confused, leading him or her to misinterpret questions or respond with inappropriate answers. Preschool children commonly distinguish between different kinds of touches, but the labels they attach to them might be different from those adults attach. Thus, they might say, "Uncle Joe touched me on my bottom," but not be aware that the meaning of that touch depends on the *context* in which it occurred. When questioning a child, a parent must elicit such context descriptions whenever possible.

One situation that should arouse some degree of suspicion occurs in custody disputes where there is already a great deal of agitation and instability, thus blurring some of the features of sexual abuse. In such cases, a child might accuse one or the other parent of abuse or neglect of some kind (physical abuse, sexual abuse, verbal abuse, neglect, and so on). Upon further analysis, such allegations might turn out to be greatly exaggerated or even completely untrue. These allegations often occur when one parent is trying to put pressure on the other or when the child wishes to simplify his or her choice and minimize his or her guilt by attacking one of the parents.

Occasionally, *contagion* episodes occur, in which one child in a group inspires others to tell the same exaggerated or untrue story about an adult or an older child toward whom the children have negative or mixed feelings. This typically occurs in a group setting, such as a day-care center or preschool, but it is highly uncommon.

Because of the potentially serious repercussions for a person unjustly accused, it is important that a parent or teacher be convinced that the child is telling the truth, based on the demonstrable features associated with sexual abuse, other evidence, and possibly witnesses. Obviously, the age and cognitive ability of the child are important considerations, as is the child's history of telling the truth. One question parents and teachers should ask themselves (but never the child) is "Does the child have anything to gain from this?" If the answer is clearly negative, that is a further indication that the child is telling the truth. If the answer is clearly positive, then the situation must be examined further.

Although younger children are not as cognitively sophisticated as older children, they are generally very truthful, especially if asked a question in an appropriate and clear manner. Adolescents present somewhat more problems because some realize the power of such accusations and use them as instruments of manipulation. If a parent or teacher suspects this is the case, he or she must carefully assess the accusations to avoid falsely accusing the alleged offender.

Despite these occasional false accusations, the vast majority of children (and adolescents) tell the truth, at least from their perspective. If a parent or teacher has any doubts after talking with the child, it is highly advisable to arrange for the child to see a counselor or therapist trained in evaluating and treating children. Such a person is better able to assess credibility and is in a more neutral position with respect to the family, thereby allowing the child a more open context for disclosure. Counseling also could prove helpful in later stages, especially if the offender denies the accusations, as the testimony of the therapist would carry great weight. Table 5–1 lists some general guidelines that parents and teachers can use to evaluate a child's accusations. If most or all of the conditions listed are present, the child is probably telling the truth and should be referred for medical and psychological examination (Nurcombe 1983). If the child's story appears suspect, the child is very inconsistent in his or her account of the incident, the child has a history of making up stories, or the child has a clear motive for lying about the alleged offender, then further discussion is indicated.

During the initial encounter, it is wise to remind the child about the importance of telling the truth, stressing that you will be entirely supportive as long as he or she does so but that you will not condone

50

Table 5-1

CHILD CREDIBILITY FACTORS

| Cognitive | Personality | Description of Events | External Evidence |
|---|---|---|---|
| Memory | Maturity level | Consistency of story over time | Witnesses |
| Intelligence | Sensitivity to others | Consistency of story across tellings to different people | Physical or medical signs |
| Logical thinking | Absence of telltale signs that the child is lying | Story the same across verbal and action (role playing or doll play) domains | Direct observation |
| Ability to distinguish fact from fantasy and lie from truth | History of honesty, especially in other emotionally charged situations | Emotional tone congruent with story | Tangible communications such as notes, letters, tapes, or drawings |
| | Presence of symptoms, signs, and effects associated with sexual abuse (see chapter 4) | Description of interactions logical and realistic, though often not completely understood | Other concrete manifestations |
| | Absence of a significant history of lying or making up stories | Child's story resistant to modification, even when confronted, pushed, prodded, or led | |
| | | Absence of important motive (other than the abuse) for attacking the alleged offender or revealing the abuse | |

lying or making up stories. Often the child starts out by telling the truth, but then becomes confused, ambivalent, and guiltridden as he or she begins to understand the seriousness of the event and the magnitude of the repercussions. At such times, the child starts to change or modify the story, resulting in increased scrutiny and general tension. An intimate, one-on-one talk is often helpful in settling the child down and clarifying this complicated picture. If a gentle confrontation does not work, it is advisable to consult a professional, particularly if you have any doubt whatsoever about whether the child is telling the truth. Many children open up to professionals in a way that is too difficult for them to handle in their family or school situation. Such professionals are often quite adept at perceiving fabrications and distortions and can more accurately evaluate the child's cognitive and memory skills.

## Assessing the Offender's Credibility

Evaluation of the alleged offender's credibility, particularly if he or she denies the incident, is also of crucial importance. In most cases, unless there is direct and irrefutable evidence, the offender will most likely deny the child's accusations, leaving parents and teachers in a quandary to what really happened and whom to believe. *In general, children are to be believed more than their alleged offenders in sexual abuse cases.* But offenders must be treated fairly and evaluated thoroughly, and their credibility should be assessed in a rigid and detailed way. The characteristics listed in table 5–1 also apply to the offender, although they must be scaled upward for age. Personal knowledge of the offender, particularly of the offender's relationship with the child, might be helpful in ascertaining which of the conflicing stories is true. If the child is able to provide details of the offender's personality, dreams, secrets, room, hobbies, quirks, body, language, actions, and so on, such information is strong evidence that the child is telling the truth.

Overall, it is much easier to assess the child than the alleged offender, as the latter is usually highly defensive and resistant to any investigation and is often in a state of emotional agitation. If a parent or teacher's attempt to communicate with the alleged offender fails, further contact and evaluation should be made by someone else, preferably a professional (Goldstein 1987).

# 6

# What to Do
# in Case of Abuse

S UPPOSE you have good reason to believe or strongly suspect that
a child has been abused, and you are in a position of authority
and caring. In addition to informing the appropriate authorities (such
as the local or state department of social services, the police department, a pediatrician, a guidance counselor, or a mental health professional) of your concerns and investigating the matter further (particularly if you know the alleged offender or are responsible for the
welfare of the child), it is important that you seek help for yourself,
especially if you find yourself overly depressed or disturbed. It is also
important that you help the child deal with the immediate stress. This
chapter describes some basic strategies to help alleviate much of the
distress experienced by the child.

## Talking to the Child

In addition to periodic discussions aimed at prevention, it is important
to be alert to the main features noted in sexually abused children as
described in the previous chapters. Even if these features are not evident, it might be worthwhile to inquire occasionally about any confusing or bad touches the child might have experienced or be experiencing at the present time. If features of abuse are apparent, it is
crucial that you talk with the child, making certain that the child feels
as relaxed and comfortable as possible. Bear in mind that sexual abuse

is a difficult and embarrassing subject for anyone, especially children, to discuss, partly because they feel anxiety and guilt about their actions and partly because they usually have been warned not to tell. Warnings and threats from the perpetrator tend to be one of two kinds: warnings that telling will result in undue harm to the perpetrator, insinuating that the child would be responsible for this; direct threats of harm or other punishments if the child informs others about what is happening. Because of these warnings and threats, children are highly reticent about offering information. They tend to be anxious, reserved, and generally uncommunicative unless they feel strong support and acceptance. Thus, it is very important that a parent, teacher, or counselor be seen as extremely caring, supportive, and accepting of the child's statements and feelings. It is also important for such a person to demonstrate a high degree of competence, stability, and direction in order for the child to feel supported and protected.

## Immediately after the Child
## Tells You What Happened

Parents typically ask, "What can I do to help my child?" The following list suggests various things you can say to the child after he or she tells you of an abusive encounter or you find out about such an encounter through other means. It is important to reassure the child by telling him or her the following:

You believe him.

She did the right thing to tell you and should not feel guilty or ashamed for telling. Assure her that you are glad that she is able to talk to you.

It was not his fault.

You are sorry it happened.

You will try your best to protect her from any future abuse. You will stay especially close to her during this time, providing extra support and nurturance.

The offender did a very bad thing, something an adult is not supposed to do to a child and something that is against the law. Do not suggest that the offender is sick or bad, as the child might have strongly ambivalent (positive and negative) feelings toward the offender. Rather, the focus should be on the behavior and the fact that the offender needs help in stopping this behavior.

You might need to take him to a doctor to make sure everything is all right.

Other adults will need to help her so it will not happen again.

You want him to see a person (like a doctor) with whom he can talk about the abusive event, the entire situation, and his feelings in a safe and private manner.

If she has any questions, she should be sure to ask. If you cannot give her the answer, you will find someone who can.

He is not dirty, bad, weird, or stupid for having been involved in the abuse.

## Stage-Related Techniques

### Infancy (Birth–1 Year)

Protect the child from any further abuse by preventing contact with the offender and reducing the number of strangers to whom the child is exposed.

Spend more time holding and cuddling the child.

Tell the child that you are sorry for what happened whether or not you think he or she can fully understand.

### Toddler and Early Childhood (2–5 Years)

Offer the child physical affection.

Answer the child's questions about the incident calmly and honestly.

Reassure the child in words and actions that he or she is safe and loved.

Talk with the child and discuss the incident. Most children welcome this, but some might be resistant. If so, do not push the child to talk about it.

Allow the child to draw or play with dolls or toys regarding the incident. This allows the child to resolve his or her anger instead of expressing it in aggressive or sexual play with friends.

Explain to the child that your talks about what happened are shared only with people who can help and are not made public knowledge.

Establish clear methods of protection, monitoring, and communication.

### Latency (6–9 Years)

Give the child love, affection, and support.

Create an open atmosphere in which you can talk with the child regarding the incident.

Give the child the opportunity to express himself or herself regarding the incident. This will alleviate much anxiety.

Provide clear boundaries and protection mechanisms.

### Preadolescence (10–12 Years)

Encourage the child to discuss the incident.

Avoid overprotection.

Keep all lines of communication open; the child might not want to talk with you about the incident at a given time. Allow the child to decide when he or she wishes to discuss it.

Consider group educational and therapy approaches.

Give the child the opportunity to talk with another trusted person if he or she cannot talk with you about the incident.

Help the child understand what happened and the possible reasons for it.

*Adolescence (13–20 Years)*

Offer the child support and the willingness to talk about the incident.

Encourage the child to seek outside professional help.

Avoid being overprotective.

Encourage group and family therapy approaches, as well as individual therapy.

Encourage the child to find out more about sexual abuse and its dynamics by reading and talking to professionals and other victims.

Give the child the opportunity to express his or her anger in appropriate ways that are not abusive to the child or others. These might include talking, drawing, or pursuing some physical activity.

Encourage the child, with the aid of a therapist, to confront the offender in an assertive and mutually helpful way.

## Medical Examination

It is important that the child be examined by a physician immediately after the disclosure of sexual abuse. This is important for protective, diagnostic, and legal reasons. Physicians are commonly involved in all abuse cases, either uncovering the abuse themselves through a routine examination or investigation of a specific (symptomatic) problem or examining the child after abuse has been uncovered through some other means. Improved medical screening techniques detect signs of abuse at a much earlier stage, so periodic checkups are of considerable importance.

During a typical exam, the physician will interview the child in a caring manner, first obtaining the child's trust and then gradually moving on to more sensitive topics. The physician will conduct a physical examination of all major body systems, focusing on oral, anal, and genital areas, particularly if sexual abuse has been previously uncovered. The physician will then perform specific tests, the nature of which will depend on the age, sex, condition, and symptoms of the child. Table 6–1 describes the tests most commonly used in three specific age/sex groups.

In addition to providing immediate medical relief from pain, injury, or infection, the physician can be very helpful in diagnosing the specific type of abuse that occurred. This could be invaluable in court proceedings, as such forensic medical testimony constitutes extremely

Table 6–1
## MEDICAL TESTING OF CHILD SEXUAL ABUSE

| Males | Prepubescent Females | Pubescent Females |
|---|---|---|
| Skin injuries | Skin injuries | Skin injuries |
| Presence of blood, semen, or sperm | Presence of blood, semen, or sperm | Presence of blood, semen, or sperm |
| Venereal infections or disease | Venereal infections or disease | Venereal infections or disease |
| Rectal or anal trauma | Rectal or anal trauma | Rectal or anal trauma |
| Rectal foreign bodies | Rectal foreign bodies | Rectal foreign bodies |
| Internal injuries | Internal injuries | Internal injuries |
| General problems in urinary, genital, or anal systems (e.g., infections, enuresis, encopresis) | General problems in urinary, genital, or anal systems (e.g., infections, enuresis, encopresis) | General problems in urinary, genital, or anal systems (e.g., infections, enuresis, encopresis) |
| Lesions, abrasions, or injuries to penis or scrotum | Bruises, abrasions, or lacerations in genital area | Bruises, abrasions, or lacerations in genital area |
| | Vaginal foreign bodies | Vaginal foreign bodies |
| | Abnormal vaginal and hymeneal openings | Pregnancy |

powerful evidence. Many sexual abuse cases do not involve forced penetration or significant physical harm, and thus are not evident in a general examination. Trained nurses and physicians, however, can detect diagnostic physical signs (such as a slight reddening, soreness, or tenderness) and even more revealing emotional or behavioral signs (such as excessive embarrassment, flinching, fear, shyness, or hesitation). Even if the physician does not discover anything, he or she can offer the child support and advice about appropriate care of his or her body and the importance of telling a trusted adult if anyone touches (or has touched) the child in private areas.

## Action-Oriented Activities

*Enhance the child's self-esteem.* Sexual abuse is an abuse of power; therefore, whether the child is a victim or an offender, he or she might feel powerless, worthless, or scared. You can do specific things at home or at school to promote the child's self-esteem and help the child feel that he or she is in control.

Communicate with the child by making a distinction between the child's intentional and forced behavior, telling the child that he or she is not responsible for the latter.

Spend time focusing on positive qualities. Ask the child what he or she likes about you then tell the child what you like about him or her.

Encourage the child to try new things. If the child makes a mistake, try not to criticize. Instead, say, "Try again, you can do it."

Take time to implement a stress-reduction program through exercise, music, art, diet, recreation, relaxation, and discussions.

Talk *with* the child, *not at* him or her.

Stimulate independence and allow the child to do things himself or herself.

Have fun together. Think of things to do together. Let the child decide on an adventure and carry it out.

Do not treat the child as a victim; this will only enhance feelings of low self-esteem.

Help the child experience *success*, *affection*, and *acceptance*, even if you must relax your standards somewhat.

These suggestions might take time to implement, but they will be rewarding for both you and the child because they build self-confidence and a strong bond that will help the child overcome his or her fears and establish positive relationships with others.

*Work through traumatic nightmares.* The child might have recurring nightmares about the trauma he or she experienced. The child might wake up screaming, crying, and so scared that he or she is unable to sleep. As a teacher and especially as a parent, you can be instrumental in helping the child work through these frightening experiences by doing some or all of the following:

Make sure the child realizes that the nightmare is not real.

Have the child draw a picture of the nightmare or tell the whole story of it.

Ask the child to describe the drawing or talk more about the story.

Ask the child to think of a way he or she can change the drawing or story to make the nightmare not scary, preferably by devising an ending in which the child feels happy and powerful.

Ask the child to make the nightmare drawing or story into an interesting but nonfrightening event.

Explain that the child does have control over dreams and that this power can be used to change nightmares so that they are not scary.

Have the child draw the nightmare, then shred the paper, put the pieces on the floor, stomp on them, and throw them away.

*Use art whenever possible.* Children love to draw. Besides being a way for them to express themselves, art also is an excellent way to reduce anxiety.

Ask the child to draw separate pictures about fear, anxiety, anger, sadness, and happiness.

Ask the child to tell you what the drawing is about. If the child resists, do not insist.

Ask the child to draw whatever he or she wants. Children often draw the abusive incident. If the child wishes to discuss the picture with you, listen but do not make judgments or offer any explanation. Just thank him or her for sharing it with you.

*Encourage writing stories or notes in a journal.* Some children respond well to writing stories or poems. If the child enjoys doing this, here is what you can do to encourage him or her:

Ask the child to write a story or poem about what it is like to be scared, angry, abused, or emotionally aroused.

Ask the child to write a story or poem about how he or she could help someone who has been a victim.

Ask the child to write a letter to the abuser. Include all that the child wants to say, but do not necessarily mail it.

*Encourage participation in drama activities.* Most children enjoy playing make-believe or pretend games. They also like dressing up and using props to act out a fantasy or some aspect of reality. Acting, role playing, and active storytelling are often helpful in working through stress. Here are some suggestions:

Ask the child to listen while you tell a story that will demonstrate how a child can avoid a potential assault. For example, a child is asked to come into a neighbor's house to see some new puppies. The child says to the neighbor, "I have to tell my parents that I'm here, then I can see your puppies." Role-play this with the child by asking him or her what he or she would do in the same situation.

Teach the child to say no by active practice and roleplaying. This might be difficult because children are often reprimanded for responding negatively to an adult. Explain that saying no in a firm tone of voice when someone tries to violate him or her is imperative in reducing the possibility of further victimization. Role-play different situations by asking the child questions to which the answer is always no.

Ask the child to say no in different ways until the child can say it firmly and with authority.

Asking older children to adopt the perpetrator role might be helpful.

Encourage participation in dramatic activities, particularly those allowing for full communication of feelings and open expression. You might want to put the child in a relatively unfamiliar role so that he or she can learn from it. For example, placing a very shy and insecure child in a role requiring overt aggression might make the child more asssertive.

Read imaginative stories aloud to the child and ask the child to pantomime the actions of one of the characters.

Involve the child in one-on-one role playing, as well as in peer groups.

Use scripts as well as more improvised play.

*Use puppets when dealing with young or resistant children.* Puppets have always intrigued children. Many animal puppets on the market today are inexpensive and might provide the child with a means of expressing and resolving his or her emotions. You can help the child make different puppets out of paper lunch bags by decorating and coloring them.

Provide dolls for the child to play with. Most children reenact the abuse incident through doll play. You also might want to play with the child to guide him or her in a direction that encourages reenacting the abuse.

Ask the child to put on a puppet show for you. If the child requests your help, give it; otherwise, be an observer.

Talk to the puppet as if the puppet has had some bad experience, including sexual abuse. Allow the child to talk for the puppet.

*Help improve the child's body image.* A child's body image often is distorted after the child is victimized. The child might feel that people see him or her as distorted, dirty, or otherwise different. The child also might be ashamed and feel empty.

Draw two outlines of the child on separate pieces of paper. Have the child fill in each with an inside and outside view. If anything is missing, ask the child to fill it in. Discuss the drawings, pointing out positive aspects of the child. Tell the child what you see on the outside as well as on the inside, stressing the fact that the child is clean, nice, good-looking and so on.

Have the child look in a full-length mirror. Ask him or her to tell you about the person in the mirror. If the child cannot respond, tell him or her what you see, emphasizing the positive. If the child responds negatively, reassure the child that even though that is how he or she might feel, that is not what you see.

*Encourage physical and social activities.* Most children like to play outdoors and mix with their peers. Following are some activities you can do to help a child work through feelings in physical ways:

Have the child hold a baseball bat, then tell the child that the ball is the abuser and that he or she can express anger by hitting the ball as hard as possible. Then ask the child how it felt to hit the ball, reinforcing the idea that the child does have power.

Some children will benefit from learning karate, which promotes self-control, power, and a sense of being prepared, protected, and powerful.

Allow the child access to outdoor play of various kinds, especially with organized groups.

## Tempering Your Own Reactions

Many parents and teachers become so caught up in their own emotions during and after the disclosure that they become highly distressed and sometimes hinder the progress of the child or the legal case against the alleged offender. It is very important for such adults to find alternative forms of relief, such as turning to people whom they trust or seeking professional counseling. Children are highly sensitive to the emotions of adults to whom they are close, especially in times of acute stress. Thus, it is vitally important that caretakers be as open, supportive, and stress-free as possible in order to nurture the child and give rational, consistent advice. Also, emotional stress can cause problems in other parts of the adult's life, including health, work, marriage, parenting of other children, and social relationships and activities. In general, it is important to work through the immediate feelings of guilt, rage, revenge, fear, and embarrassment to be most productive.

## Other Systems

Be aware of the effects of the disclosure on other people in the family system, as well as in the school and community systems. Decide who is to know about the abuse and when and how you will inform them. Also help the child deal with the effects caused by making the abuse public. Pay special attention to siblings, friends, and classmates. Use this opportunity to discuss sexual abuse and what children can do to protect themselves. Help children say no in assertive ways, especially to adults who attempt to scare, bribe, or seduce them. Describe the steps they should take and the people they should contact in case they are approached by potentially abusive people.

# 7

# General Problems
# and Treatment Goals

A LTHOUGH each case is different, certain common problems routinely and almost inevitably arise in all cases where sexual abuse has occurred. The particular pattern of problems might be different in terms of intensity and duration, but the concerns discussed in this chapter are encountered in all cases.

## Anxiety

Before Jill revealed the "special game" her uncle had taught her, she was observed by parents and teachers to have become increasingly nervous and high-strung. She was both cautious and hesitant in her remarks and often reacted oversensitively to minor incidents and fairly neutral comments. She had trouble falling asleep at night and frequently awoke during the night because of disturbing dreams. To the surprise of her parents, Jill's anxiety did not diminish after she disclosed the abuse; in fact, her problems appeared to get worse.

Anxiety is a universal characteristic associated with stress of any kind. As such, it is probably the best indicator of some kind of disturbance, although anxiety in and of itself must be examined in terms of its source and context. In sexual abuse cases, anxiety stems from a number of sources: (1) fear of having done something wrong, (2) confusion about what has been happening, and (3) fear and uncertainty about negative consequences, especially in regard to revealing the secret. Anxiety represents a type of inner flooding in which emotions are stronger than thoughts and, as such, are virtually uncontrollable. The person cannot act and feels generally confused. It is, therefore, of the utmost importance to help reduce the child's anxiety by offering ways of cognitively and actively handling problems.

*Focus of Help.* Decrease anxiety by giving clear and rational answers about questions and concerns, as well as by inspiring a sense of confidence and security in terms of future consequences. It is extremely important that the child gain a stronger feeling of self-control.

## Immobilization

Ben is a ten-year-old boy who was sexually molested by an elderly man who lived on the next block. The man was known to be very fond of children and often invited them to his house. For several months, Ben and this man enjoyed many activities together, both inside and outside the man's house. About a month before the abuse was uncovered, however, the man started fondling Ben in various ways. Ben was confused about what to do, especially in light of the many moments of joy he shared with this man and the overall friendly context in which the multiple abuse incidents occurred. Ben appeared to be in a trance most of the time, almost as if he were drinking liquor or using drugs. He became morosely silent and was almost completely unresponsive to things and activities that had previously interested him.

Immobilization represents a particular form of anxiety, one that impedes almost all areas of functioning. The child is left virtually incapacitated, not knowing what to think, feel, or do. Although the sexual abuse is the initial cause, immobilization soon moves into other areas of functioning that relate to interpersonal contact. The child typically appears to be in a trance and acts in a robotic or zombie-like way, performing normal functions only under some pressure.

Even more than with general anxiety, it is imperative that parents and professionals assist the child in gaining power, particularly in regard to actions directly related to the sexual abuse. Only with a sense of self-control and power will the child be able to overcome this immobility.

*Focus of Help.* Encourage the child to act in a positive, controlled, and fully informed way throughout the crisis, constantly pushing him or her to become or remain involved in many types of activities.

## Shock

Bert, a twelve-year-old boy, confessed to having been sexually abused by his mother when he was a young child. Bert admitted that he was shocked by the incident itself and even more so by the memory and admission of it. In fact, he constantly broke down into tears at the memory.

Particularly in cases in which there has been a strong personal bond with clear role expectations in terms of duties and responsibilities, sexual abuse comes as a shock. Shock can often resemble or lead to immobilization, but shock usually represents an almost complete withdrawal from feelings and the energy needed to act in a healthy manner. Shock is a by-product of any personal trauma, and in its transitory form, it is a healthy response to sexual abuse. In cases such as the one described above, however, the state of shock has become a way of life, particularly in regard to the abuse incident itself and the circumstances associated with it. Unfortunately, these associated circumstances have a way of increasing over time, to the point where a person is incapacitated in almost every form of social interaction. Dealing with shock first and foremost requires a high degree of honesty and courage. The victim must accept that abuse occurred and have the courage to believe that he or she can live with it.

*Focus of Help.* Help the child to become more aware of the sexual abuse and learn to accept the fact that it happened. It is crucial that the child own up to the event and proceed accordingly. Expressive actions and open discussions are generally helpful in recognizing and working through the trauma of sexual abuse, although care must be taken that the child's behavior is under some form of control.

## Sadness and Depression

Jane was seventeen when she was discovered in bed with her father. After extensive interviews, she confessed that she and her father had been sexually involved for the past six years. She always felt extremely close to her father and he to her, giving her many privileges that her siblings did not receive. Although she was eventually relieved of the burden of keeping her affair a secret, Jane became profoundly depressed by the experience, attempting to kill herself on three occasions before she was placed in a more secure setting.

Sadness is a universal affect associated with any kind of loss. If sexual abuse is couched in what was perceived to be a positive framework, and especially if the victim has strong positive feelings of affection or respect for the adult involved, it is almost inevitable that sadness will emerge as a powerful aftereffect. To the extent that something special happened between the people, however exploitive it might have been, there is bound to be a marked sense of loss, leading to feelings of sadness and perhaps depression. Such a loss, however, does not have to be forever, as the two people might establish a healthy relationship at a later date. For the present, however, it is important that a parent respect the child's sense of loss, while attempting to provide a healthier, more optimistic outlook.

*Focus of Help.* Expect and accept a child's experience of loss and subsequent sadness, while helping the child distance himself or herself from the experience and perpetrator. This will enhance the child's self-esteem and the possibility that he or she will be able to establish a healthy relationship with the perpetrator as well as with other people.

Intimacy must, however, be directed more toward more appropriate objects of affection.

## Anger

Susan was molested by her stepfather for almost a year before anyone would believe her outcries. She had told her mother on several occasions, but was harshly criticized each time, accused of lying, and warned never to speak of such matters again. Finally, she revealed her experiences to the school guidance counselor, who initiated immediate and direct action. Susan's bitterness toward both her stepfather and her mother erupted after this revelation and the consequent investigation, as she repeatedly spoke of her hatred for both of them and her desire not to have any contact with them whatsoever.

Closely akin to sadness in that it is stimulated by a sense of loss, anger commonly follows sadness in terms of coping with sexual abuse. Such anger might take extreme forms, including feelings of absolute hatred or severe behavioral outbursts. Although it feels more uncomfortable to be around a person who is extremely angry, anger is usually a healthier sign than depression, since anger represents a form of stubborn self-preservation and at least some attempt at control and boundary maintenance. Anger is also a distancing mechanism, an emotion that allows the victim to gain the necesary physical and psychological distance from the perpetrator, thereby providing both a measure of protection and a feeling of autonomy and independence.

*Focus of Help.* Allow and encourage the expression of anger without making moralistic judgments or unduly criticizing a child's angry stance or behavior. Naturally, it is important that there be clear limits as to what is permitted, for the child's and the parents' sake. Within those limits, however, anger should be encouraged as a way to distance oneself from the situation and to provide an important release of pent-up feelings.

## Guilt

After being in psychotherapy for a year and a half, Alice, a thirty-five-year-old woman, finally confessed that she had been sexually abused by her uncle when she was in the third and fourth grades. Despite his protestations and warnings to the contrary, Alice always felt a profound sense of shame and guilt about the matter, strongly believing that she was committing a sin and acting immorally. Alice had carried a strong sense of guilt with her since that time, a feeling that significantly interfered with all her heterosexual relationships. She had sought therapeutic help because of chronic problems in sustaining relationships and enjoying sexuality, never realizing the connection with the abuse.

Guilt in sexual abuse cases is highly complex, and it is of two kinds. First, most children feel that there is something wrong with their engaging in such intimate behavior with an adult. This is often enhanced by admonishments not to tell the secret of their special play. Obviously, most older children and adolescents consciously know that engaging in such sexual activity violates a strong taboo in the family, religion, and general culture. This persistent and nagging sense that they are participating in an action that is immoral and even sinful represents one form of guilt.

Another sense of guilt comes from feelings of having betrayed one or more people. If the child does not tell, the child feels as though he or she is betraying a parent or other adult who either should be aware of the incident or has a separate intimate relationship with the perpetrator. Alternatively, if the child eventually does reveal the truth, the child has betrayed the particularly powerful and ambivalent relationship he or she has had with the perpetrator. This often stems from the fact that the perpetrator has forced the child to promise not to tell and has warned that bad things will happen to the perpetrator if the child does tell.

These two major sources of guilt are commonly experienced by victims, with the unfortunate result that many are unwilling or reluctant to fully disclose what has happened to them.

*Focus of Help.* Affirm that what happened was wrong but that it was not the child's fault. The blame falls on the adult, who clearly should have known better. It is also important to help the child talk about the experience and to review her or his role in the abuse, with the intention of preventing future occurrences by teaching the child to act in a more assertive and self-protective manner.

Incidentally, some degree of guilt might not be harmful or misplaced, particularly in relation to adolescents who might have engaged in seductive activities for reasons of manipulation, power, and control. In such cases, the adolescent must review his or her role in the situation and confess his or her part in the activities. It still should be stressed, however, that most of the fault lies with the adult perpetrator.

## Stigma

For more than three weeks after his disclosure of sexual abuse by his mother's current boyfriend, John refused to go to school, claiming that he felt sick in the morning and complaining that other children picked on him at school. When questioned further about his feelings, John described at least three other children who had found out about the sexual abuse and had made snide remarks to him. John believed that most of the school knew about his unfortunate experiences and that he was labeled as being "weird" and "queer."

It is common for children to be immensely concerned about their reputation or status with others (particularly peers and friends) once sexual abuse has been made public. Even with very private cases in which information is highly protected and confidentiality guarded in all respects, it is highly likely that some information or, perhaps worse, rumors will be circulated within a short time. Since gossip travels fast, it is realistic to expect that many others will have at least some knowledge of what has happened to the child. The child, confronted by this knowledge in the form of direct comments and indirect behaviors, often feels negatively labeled and stigmatized. In turn, the child typically tries to retaliate or attempts to escape the source of stress. To the extent that the source of stress is an important activity in the child's life (such as school), such withdrawal could have serious secondary consequences.

*Focus of Help.* Admit to the child that other people probably do know something about what happened but probably not nearly as much as the child believes. Moreover, such knowledge does not necessarily lead to rejection or ridicule; more frequently, it is the source of interest and titillation. As such, the child can exercise great power in controlling the manner in which other people treat him or her by acting in a positive and confident way and certainly not accepting the labels in any manner whatsoever, whether in thought or action.

## Ambivalence

Melissa, a seven-year-old girl, was told by her brother that if she wanted to play with him and his male friend, she would have to do certain things for them, such as taking off her clothes, allowing them to touch her genitals, and in turn touching theirs. Admiring her brother and wanting to spend more time with him and his friend, while at the same time knowing that what he proposed was very wrong, Melissa had strongly mixed feelings, which caused her a great amount of stress and severe stomachaches. In fact, her stomach problems escalated until she was finally able to talk to her father about her brother's proposal.

It is not uncommon for children to have two or more conflicting feelings in regard to the sexual abuse. Lacking the means to resolve such powerful ambivalence, children become intensely confused and distressed. Ambivalence is particularly hard to deal with if the feelings are of an apparently contradictory nature, such as love and anger or loyalty and betrayal. Although multiple emotions are both predictable and healthy in the long run, they are particularly hard to handle in the short run.

*Focus of Help.* Assist the child in learning to accept his or her multiple feelings, while at the same time working toward a more integrated method of experiencing emotions and especially an integrated way of expressing emotions in action. It might be important at first to help the child become more aware of his or her mixed feelings by gently probing and inquiring into various areas of concern. The child should be told that all feelings are legitimate expressions of personal experience and that there is nothing wrong or unusual in having mixed feelings about such a traumatic event.

## Fear

Penny had been petrified about talking to investigators from the police department and social service agencies, even though her teacher had discovered Penny's diary, reporting in detail the multiple abuses by her next-door cousin. Her cousin, who was three years older than Penny (she was sixteen and he nineteen) had an extensive reputation for being a bully and for being extremely short-tempered; he was also an accomplished weight lifter and had a brown belt in karate. Only when Penny moved to another state, where she lived with very protective relatives, was she able to mention her cousin's extreme threats on her life. She had refused to disclose the abuse precisely for that reason, and she was still observed to be inordinately cautious, secretive, sensitive, scared, and paranoid, even after several months in her new home more than a thousand miles away. She would often wake up during the night claiming that she heard strange sounds or noises outside, and she had frequent nightmares about her cousin finding her. Although the court had prohibited her cousin from having contact with her, he sent her a death threat letter, which Penny unfortunately read. Even though he was subsequently put in jail for the sexual abuse of Penny and other girls, Penny remained excessively afraid of her cousin, fearing that he was going to break out of jail and subsequently rush to attack her.

Extreme fear or terror is experienced less frequently than many of the other emotions. It is typically experienced when the abuser makes direct threats of violence if the victim were to reveal any of the sexual encounters. Despite the relative infrequency of extreme fear, most children are at least somewhat afraid of what the perpetrator might do to them, sometimes making up fantasies that are far worse than reality. When these fantasies are reinforced by actual statements or threats, the feelings of fear become even more powerful.

*Focus of Help.* Help the child to talk about specific fears and make clear, realistic, and enforceable plans for circumventing the fear or preventing the fear from materializing. It is often important that certain boundaries be established and monitored and that support and protection be clearly provided to the victim. If necessary, the court will issue a restraining order, particularly if there has been a direct threat of violence or a history of violent behavior on the part of the perpetrator. It is of the utmost importance that children be surrounded by people they trust and can count on for protection.

## Betrayal

Jim had realized for more than two months that his older brother, Sam, was molesting a young retarded girl who lived in the neighborhood. Although Jim and Sam frequently did things together, Jim felt it important to inform his parents about Sam's doings. Before this happened, however, Jim approached Sam with his intentions. Hearing them, Sam admonished Jim not to be a tattletale and traitor and assured Jim that what he was doing was perfectly all right because no force was involved. According to Sam, this neighborhood girl got really turned-on by the sexual play and was a very eager partner. After much careful thought, Jim still decided to tell his parents, believing that the girl in question was of extremely limited intelligence and probably was not aware of what she was doing. Jim did inform on his brother, but he felt at the time, and continued to feel for several months afterward, a deep sense of having betrayed a person very close to him.

Betrayal often accompanies guilt as an emotion, but it often has social and cultural roots as well. Many children feel a strong sense of loyalty to people close to them, particularly other family members, and experience feelings of betrayal when they are forced to disclose family problems to the outside world. Moreover, children are frequently taught (by adults and especially by peers) that squealing and tattle-tailing are not actions in which they should engage, particularly if they have a special friendship or sense of loyalty or camaraderie with the other person. The protocol for sexual abuse cases, however, calls for a full confession of all the details, however sordid they might be. Matters are made far worse when one or more members of the immediate family rush to the perpetrator's defense, thereby splitting the family into rival factions. The victim then receives the double message that telling was both acceptable and unacceptable; this causes much stress and an enduring feeling that telling was not worth the problems doing so caused.

*Focus of Help.* Assist the child in recognizing that what he or she did was very important and healthy, despite what others might insinuate or say. It also might be important to intervene directly with other family members to regain family unity. Failing that, efforts should be made to involve the family in therapy.

## Repression

At fifty-two years of age, Doug was fired from his fourth job and sank even deeper into his chronic alcoholism. Upon placement in an alcohol retreat, Doug experienced many flashbacks of childhood experiences, one of which was a particularly traumatic and vicious sexual assault by a stranger who had offered him a ride. Not knowing what to do and being warned off any direct action by the man who raped him, Doug became intensely confused for a day or so and then promptly forgot the incident. For the most part, he was successful in his attempts at forgetting, and he found in later years that drinking aided his attempts to forget or ignore the past.

Most people try to forget unpleasant events as much as possible. Unfortunately, the distress associated with such events is usually far too powerful to ignore, causing emotional or behavioral side effects. Occasionally, however, a situation occurs that is either too traumatic or too much out of the ordinary for a person to digest and accept as his or her own experience. The person is likely to repress such an event because he or she cannot consciously deal with it in a productive manner. Many people hope that the adage "out of sight, out of mind" will hold, but repression rarely works cleanly and smoothly, typically leaving some dramatic gaps and vulnerabilities. When these surface, the trauma returns, causing intense distress unless actively treated.

*Focus of Help.* Assist the child in remembering and dealing with the sexual abuse rather than forgetting or ignoring the problem. It is crucial that the child work through the problem rather than try to avoid or escape it.

## Incomprehension

Mark, ten years old, simply could not believe that his uncle, a former Marine captain, could have engaged in such behavior with him. The uncle had invited Mark over to play a new video game on the computer. While Mark was there, his uncle had made an explicit sexual overture to Mark, showing him various pornographic pictures of men and boys together and proceeding to fondle Mark's genitals. Mark immediately told his parents what had happened and held up extremely well during the subsequent investigation, even though his uncle strongly denied all the allegations. Although Mark's relationship with his uncle cooled down noticeably following the investigation, Mark was continually haunted by the question of why his uncle had done this. Mark simply could not believe that his uncle was capable of such actions and had no way of understanding them.

Children and adolescents of all ages often fail to understand the complex reasons why an adult (or any person who should know better) actively initiates sexual contact with them. This state of incomprehension is usually of minor intensity, especially as compared with the more powerful emotions described above, but in certain cases it can reach a substantial magnitude. In particular, children who tend to internalize stress, as well as more intelligent or verbal children who require rational or logical answers, are noticeably taken aback by most episodes of sexual abuse. Given that the dynamics of sexual abuse are extremely complex and difficult even for therapists to untangle, it is no wonder that children and other family members are often extremely puzzled and mystified by the occurrence of such actions.

*Focus of Help.* Assist the child in arriving at some form of psychological understanding of what happened. This understanding should be geared to the child's intellectual level, stage of development, and degree of psychological sophistication. It is not necessary to learn the total truth about this situation; what is most important is to help the child acquire a feeling of understanding and some (partial) truth concerning what happened.

## Sexual Preoccupation

When she was twelve years old, two years after the last known encounter with her father, Nancy became extremely interested in boys, valuing her contact with them much more highly than any other endeavor in her life. These relationships invariably became highly sexualized, with Nancy experiencing what she reported as "strange and thrilling feelings at the same time" when she engaged in sexual play. Despite the advice and warnings of her friends, Nancy refused to use birth control consistently and soon became pregnant. Although she quickly had an abortion, she felt very sad afterward. Unfortunately, this episode did not prevent her from repeating the same pattern in five subsequent relationships. Finally, at age fourteen, she ran away from home and decided to have a baby.

Intense concern and preoccupation with sex is the most universal and flagrant characteristic of sexual abuse cases. This preoccupation, however, can take many forms, ranging from overt and incessant public masturbation on the one hand to extreme fear and frigidity or impotence on the other. In most cases, the sexual channel is affected in various ways by the abuse, both in present functioning and in subsequent functioning. Memories of previous sexual abuse often are resurrected when more normal sexual channels are triggered (such as in adolescence, intimacy, or marriage), causing much tension and ambivalence. The early exposure to adult sexuality also confuses children, often causing gross misperceptions about sexuality itself, as well as a pervasive sense of anxiety and excitement about it.

*Focus of Help.* Clarify normal expressions and boundaries of sexuality and review basic knowledge and values associated with sex. Help the child not to engage in sexual activity that is either too overt or too unplanned, as both types of activity can lead to serious negative consequences. The child should not be told that sexuality and sexual play are wrong, but that there are moral, social, religious, and family rules that apply. It is also helpful to consult a pediatrician or nurse who can clarify the biological aspects of sexuality and provide some basic counseling.

## Generalization

Terry, a fifteen-year-old girl who was forced to engage in oral sex with one of her male teachers, became extremely afraid of attending school and developed an intense loathing of all adult men. Terry even developed an intense distrust of her father, with whom she had been very close, and a strong disgust toward him. She frequently criticized pornography of all kinds, as well as various ads she saw in newspapers and on television, and she told her parents that she hoped they were not engaging in the "disgusting acts of beasts."

When the abuse has been very severe, or when the victim is extremely sensitive, it is likely that the child will develop some form of generalization after the specific abuse has been dealt with. Although the forms of generalization vary, all victims who generalize extend their feelings or opinions regarding sexual abuse into other, often more normal and more neutral, contexts. A child might sincerely believe that no adult is to be trusted, that all men have dirty minds, and that the whole world is laughing at them behind their backs.

*Focus of Help.* Assist the child in dealing with the specific sexual abuse incidents and the associated secondary consequences, but help him or her not to extend feelings of revulsion to other, more remote contexts, at least not without strong evidence. As a rule, the one important way to deal with generalization is to consider it a form of prejudice and to treat it accordingly, however traumatic the precipitating event might have been. It is also important to remind children of the boundaries of the problem, that things are not just black and white, and that people can act in different ways. Overall, it is important that children understand that human actions are complex and that not all people are the same.

## Victimization

Toby told the police about the films a friend's brother (Bob, age twenty-one) was making of many of the neighborhood girls and boys. These films were pornographic, with children being lured into a specifically equipped room with promises of various treats. Before telling his parents, Toby had told his friend, who quickly warned his brother. In turn, Bob had destroyed or removed most of the evidence and had substantially changed the layout and equipment in his basement.

In the subsequent investigation, Toby revealed that he himself had been molested by yet another neighborhood boy when he was younger but that he had been afraid to tell. Toby's friend and his older brother strongly denied Toby's allegations, and they gathered a group of people who not only testified to Bob's innocence, but also directly attacked Toby's credibility as an honest, intelligent person. Bob also approached several of the other children in question, offering them rewards if they kept matters secret and issuing dire warnings about what would happen if they were to tell.

Although investigators were able to uncover inconsistencies in the stories of Bob and his younger brother, they did not have enough evidence to take matters further. In addition to losing their friendship, Toby was treated rudely and coldly by almost all his previous friends. He was labeled a "squealer" by even his most trusted friends and called far worse names by other people. Toby began to have fights with his peers and to experience severe problems in school, both academically and behaviorally.

Unfortunately, one of the main consequences of being a victim of sexual abuse is a tendency to victimize other people. The victim fulfills a need to work through the abuse experience by repeating it and projecting it onto others. These victims become extremely vulnerable to problems of various kinds and are often regarded as seriously disturbed.

*Focus of Help.* Assist the child in learning appropriate, thorough, and therapeutic expressions of events and feelings and help the child develop adult and peer support systems. It also might be helpful to instruct the child in specific techniques of handling peer pressure and criticism. In addition, the critics themselves might be asked, in both individual and group situations, about their reasons for so acting, helping them look at the broader picture.

Not all children manifest all these problems. Children typically display three or four main stances during the course of the abuse, often only one at any given time. Since the range of responses is quite wide, however, it is important for parents and teachers to be aware of the possible responses and to regard each response both as a diagnostic cue that something has happened and as the child's attempt, however feeble or primitive, to cope with the stress involved.

# 8

# The Family Web

F AMILIES play an important part in sexual abuse, either as the source of the abuse or as a support system during the ordeal following disclosure. Sometimes, as in the case of a family that seeks help through therapy, it can even be a combination of both. In this chapter, we concentrate on incestuous families.

The absolute number, frequency, and relative proportion of incest cases continue to increase. It has been labeled the "hidden epidemic" and the "best-kept secret," although recently it has been gaining more attention. Father-daughter and stepfather-daughter incest is the most common type, followed by sibling incest; sexual abuse initiated by mothers, once thought to be extremely uncommon (less than 1 percent) also is being reported more often. Incest appears to occur far more frequently in blended families, with incidence of stepfather-daughter incest reported to be up to seven times as much as biological father-daughter incest cases (Russell 1986). If the definition of incest is expanded to include relatives with whom the family has regular contact (uncles, aunts, grandparents, cousins, and so on), as well as the myriad connections with steprelatives, the number of cases reaches staggering levels.

Together with cases of physical abuse, the high number of incest cases makes domestic crime the most prevalent, though perhaps the most underreported, of all crimes against people. Fortunately, with increasing awareness of the problem, scrutiny of children, and the mandate to inform whenever abuse is suspected, cases that would previously have gone undetected are being discovered. It is likely, however, that a large number of cases still go unreported and unde-tected, causing many short-term and long-term problems (Sanford 1980).

Understanding family functioning is essential to understanding in-cest, as incest is indeed a family affair in the worst sense. Although there is no such thing as a typical incestuous family, several general characteristics apply. However, it should be stressed that incestuous families exist with members acting quite differently from those de-scribed below. For the purposes of this discussion, we will focus on the most prevalent scenarios, those of father-daughter incest and sib-ling incest, and then consider incest involving a somewhat more dis-tant relative.

## Father-Daughter Incest

In incest between a father and daughter, the *father* typically plays a dominant role in the house, particularly in regard to decision making. He is considered to be very powerful, moody, temperamental, and strong willed. He rarely expresses tenderness or empathy, tending to be absorbed in daily tasks and duties. He is often highly moralistic, opinionated, and prejudiced, especially of people adopting different lifestyles. He has strong opinions concerning morals and values, often dogmatically declaring principles of action that others in the family are to follow.

The *mother* is characteristically passive and weak, attending to basic duties in the household but allowing her husband to have a relatively free reign in terms of power and control. She is often aware of her husband's close relationships with the children, although she is rarely aware of the actual abuse. She tends not to delve too deeply into such matters, however, remaining somewhat aloof. Many abused children claim that on one or more occasions they tried to tell their mother about what was going on, but the mother either refused to believe them or minimized the problem. Occasionally the reverse dynamics of a very powerful and controlling mother along with a weak, needy, and overly dependent father are observed. At one time, this was thought to be the most common set of dynamics, but more recent investigations suggest this is not the case (Herman 1981).

Given these characteristics, it is not surprising that the parents' marriage is seriously disturbed. In fact, it can be argued that the real (that is, the psychological) marriage is between the father and the daughter, with the father's moralism preventing him from going outside the family for satisfaction, such as by having an affair.

The *daughter* who becomes the victim of sexual abuse is frequently singled out by the father as being special and is given an unusually high degree of status and responsibility by both parents. Such a girl becomes an "executive child," one who acts as a virtual coequal with the mother in many arenas. In fact, it can be argued that the sexual involvement between the father and the daughter represents yet one more manifestation of this change in status. Abused daughters often are intensely ambivalent about the abuse, feeling that it is wrong but also feeling under a great deal of pressure from the father, pressure not to tell and pressure to retain their special relationship. Ambivalence reaches a maximum in cases where the abuse is felt to be an expression of love or privilege and no overt force is involved, yet the daughter (and sometimes the father) still has a pervasive feeling of discomfort or wrongdoing. The daughter deeply cares for her father and does not want to see him get hurt or punished, but she also realizes that what is happening is wrong.

*Siblings* in such families play a variety of roles. Younger daughters will often be additional or future victims, whereas sons tend to be antagonistic to, and distant from, the father. In a number of incestuous families, the nonvictimized boys exhibit problems both at home and at school, typically of an aggressive or antiauthority nature.

The *family* as a whole tends to be severely isolated from other families and from community activities in general. Parents are often highly critical of other adults and families, preferring to stay at home rather than get involved in activities or functions outside the family. The following general characteristics of the incestuous family have been identified.

## Characteristics of the Incestuous Family

*Blurred Boundaries.* Parent and child levels are inadequately separated, with normal role definitions and distinctions being extremely unclear. Members are highly enmeshed.

*Role Reversal.* In many cases, the incest victim is cast in the executive child role of a parent, housekeeper, and mate. The legal mate is often relegated to the status of a naive and powerless child.

*Isolation.* The family refrains from contact with outsiders and is often suspicious, distrustful, and even antagonistic about genuine contact or intimacy with outsiders.

*Lack of Privacy.* Within the family, there is little privacy for members, either physically or psychologically. Members often invade each other's rooms and personal possessions, viewing attempts at privacy as an attack on the family. Sometimes doors are left open or even removed, and even bathrooms cannot be locked.

*Mishandling of Power.* Power in incestuous families is often highly distorted, concentrated far more in one parent (the perpetrator) than the other. Moreover, power is abused quite frequently, particularly in regard to the abuse and the interactions surrounding it.

*Low Self-esteem.* The incestuous family generally considers itself extremely weak and needy, relying on itself because outsiders are too threatening.

*Fear of Breaking Up.* The enmeshment of the incestuous family, along with the tacit acceptance of abuse, is supported in large part by the family's fear of disintegration, a fear greater than the distress engendered by the abuse.

*Lack of Assertiveness and Independence.* Members of incestuous families are extremely dependent on each other, with assertiveness in action and anger in emotion singularly absent in most intrafamily encounters.

*Poor Concentration.* Despite its enmeshment, the family does not allow full communication within itself, chiefly due to its distorted role boundaries and its difficulty in accepting and expressing anger and independence.

*Rigidity.* The family often espouses a strongly conventional moral code, superficially adhered to in dogmatic ways. Family activities and management are typically characterized by a high degree of rigidity.

*Lack of Appropriate Sympathy.* Family members mainly care for themselves and are not able to understand or cope with the feelings and needs of other family members.

*Denial.* Members of the incestuous family (especially the perpetrator) typically deny that they have any problems and refuse to admit that the outside world has anything of value to offer.

*Secrecy.* The family often has glaring secrets concerning the outside lives and private fantasies of members, as well as the big secret of the incest itself.

### After the Disclosure

When incest is uncovered, it has major repercussions for all family members. Fathers in such families typically take one of two courses of action: They either vehemently deny that any sexual abuse has occurred, or they abjectly confess to the offense. In most cases, confession occurs only if there is overwhelming evidence that cannot be validly denied or repudiated by the father or if the father was himself very upset (or at least ambivalent) about the abuse, almost setting things up so he would get caught. In situations where there is marginal or vague evidence, particularly when it is the word of the child versus the word of the father, many fathers deny any such involve-

ment, harshly criticizing the child for telling lies or spreading un-
founded rumors. It should be recognized, however, that children in
intact families rarely lie about such matters, suggesting that such allegations should be taken very seriously. Even in the unlikely circum-
stance that actual sexual abuse did not occur, the making of such
allegations is a sign of major family dysfunction. As such, any allegation should be discussed within the family and with a counselor or
therapist outside the family.

The revelation of sexual abuse is a significant step in realigning
family boundaries. At last, the secret has been revealed, carrying with
it the implication that the old coalitions are not effective and, indeed,
not wanted. By itself, this produces a crisis in the family that is more
subtle, yet more dramatic, than the revelation itself (Mayer 1983).
Specifically, at least four glaring questions are brought into focus for
the whole family:

1. What has been the relationship between the father and daughter
   (victim)?
2. What does this have to say about the parents' past, present, and
   future marital relationship?
3. What does this have to say about the mother, both in terms of
   her not knowing about the abuse and in terms of her roles as a
   wife, mother, guardian, and so on?
4. What effect does this have on other members of the family?

These four questions come immediately to the fore, often in confused and indirect ways. Typically, the father becomes extremely defensive or withdrawn, while the mother becomes extraordinarily
tense, confused, and agitated. Meanwhile, the daughter characteristically becomes acutely ambivalent about her actions, particularly when
other systems are brought into play and family members (especially
her parents) become increasingly upset. The girl often feels guilty,
upset, and sorry that her parents are suffering such pain and turmoil.
During this phase, it is common for the daughter to retract her statements, at least to some extent, thereby trying to minimize the nega-

tive impact. This attempt at softening the blow only increases tension and heightens confusion. Moreover, such daughters are more harshly criticized and scrutinized by all parties, resulting in much more strain on them.

Perhaps the greatest stress is experienced within the parents' marriage, as the revelation of incest is a blow to the integrity of the marriage bond. Incest represents an affair by the husband, a violation of age/generation boundaries, and a violation of the moral code under which families are supposed to live. Incest thus delivers a triple blow to a marriage, typically engendering rage, disgust, and withdrawal on the part of the wife. To the extent that the wife feels at all to blame for the incest or as negligent in her duty to protect her children and the sanctity of her family, she may herself experience extreme anxiety and depression. All this results in major marital friction, often leading to voluntary or involuntary separation.

The husband, busy trying to defend himself against allegations he claims are untrue, has to face the angry outbursts and stony silence of his wife, causing him to become extremely anxious, agitated, and depressed. His performance at work frequently suffers, as does his ability to maintain involvement in outside activities and interpersonal relationships. Similarly, all other family members, both in the immediate family and in the extended family, become confused and agitated, not knowing which course of action the family (and society) will take.

Precisely because the family is in such turmoil, it is extremely important for it to seek outside professional help. Preferably, such support should come from someone trained in dealing with family crises, someone who will support the feelings of each family member but also take steps to ensure that immediate protection is given to the victim and appropriate services are rendered to the family. In most cases, once incest between a father and a daughter who are living in the same home has been reported, one or the other of them (usually the father) is forced to separate from the home for an unspecified period of time. During that time, further evaluations are made and plans for treatment are begun.

If the allegations are substantiated and the father is found guilty, the court will rule accordingly, sometimes sentencing the father to prison for a period of time. The terms of the sentencing depend a great deal on the circumstances surrounding the sexual abuse, including frequency, intensity, type of action, number of people affected, use of direct force or aggression, and physical pain. If the offense is *relatively* mild, the court might not sentence the father to prison but instead require both the father and daughter to participate in individual therapy, with the father paying for both his own and his daughter's services. Group and family therapy also might be required.

Although the revelation of incest occasionally causes the breakup of a marriage, more often it strengthens the marriage in direct and indirect ways, both positive and negative. In many cases, the mother has a strong alliance with her husband, tending to believe him over her daughter, even despite glaring evidence to the contrary. Thus, she tends to side with her husband against her daughter, in effect isolating the daughter from the inner family. This indirectly strengthens the marriage, but at the expense of losing a child and destroying a vital bond of trust.

A more positive route exists if the mother trusts the credibility of her daughter's account, often with the assistance of a counselor, caseworker, or other child advocate. Although this puts a strain on the marriage, it often provides the power these mothers need to forge a more equal and viable marital bond, one that will result in more intimacy for both partners, as well as ensure more protection for the children. This represents a major challenge for both marriage partners, one that requires a careful look at their marriage, both in terms of past dynamics that might have indirectly encouraged or allowed the incest to occur and in terms of paying careful attention to present and future ways of improving the marriage. Care must be taken, however, not to view the incest as a result of any problem or vacuum in the marriage. Rather, the marriage should be looked at as a potential resource in terms of prevention and communication.

It must be stressed that incest is primarily the problem of the perpetrator, regardless of how many other factors affected his feelings and consequent actions. It is essential that perpetrators be held accountable for their actions and not be allowed to blame them on problems caused by marriage, work, alcohol use, interpersonal relationships, money, and so on. Obviously, these and other problems often make people vulnerable and distressed in a number of ways, but just as highly aggressive or homocidal behavior is not condoned as a way of reducing stress, sexual offenses should not be condoned or excused for these reasons.

## Sibling Incest

Another kind of family incest, representing about 20 to 25 percent of reported incest cases, is that between siblings, typically between an older brother and a younger sister (all combinations are reported, with brother-sister incest being by far the most prevalent). This type of incest is probably dramatically underreported, much more so than that between a parent and a child. The reasons for this are complicated, but probably are related to the difficulty in distinguishing between normal sexual play and sexually abusive encounters.

Young children frequently have little idea of acceptable versus unacceptable sexual behavior with siblings. This is in sharp distinction to sexual interplay with their parents, which children typically realize is much more unusual and questionable. Younger children are often told by older siblings that such sexual play is normal but should be kept secret. This further confuses the younger child. Occasionally, younger children consider sexual involvement an honor that allows them to engage in more adultlike play with older siblings.

In addition, there is often a strong sibling bond that stresses loyalty and acts against squealing. Even though siblings frequently squeal on each other regarding much more petty endeavors, such as borrowing one another's possessions, calling each other names, or pushing or hitting each other, they often remain loyal to each other in more powerful situations. To the extent that they have to live much more with each other in day-to-day contact (including school) than they do with their parents, children often hesitate before betraying their siblings.

Another factor that mediates against reporting is the frequent threat of force used by older brothers, a threat that younger children perceive as being quite real, as they have experienced its effects in other matters in the past. Contrary to the more subtle psychological force employed by fathers, children are often physically afraid of their older siblings.

As a consequence of these forces, both the allure and pressure surrounding sibling incest are significant. Thus, most sibling incest cases go unreported for extremely long periods of time, with many cases not being shared with other people until the victims themselves are adults. Victims often share their experiences with their mate or therapist only as a result of chronic tension or problems in their marriage or other relationships.

Despite its widespread occurrence, incest between siblings probably has a less severe effect on the family than incest between a parent and a child. Whereas parent-child incest shatters both generational and authority boundaries, sibling incest at least occurs within the same generational level, thereby preserving the normal parent-child bonds of unconditional trust and acceptance. Despite these differences, however, sibling incest is still a serious matter, as it is a deliberate violation of the younger child's body, a violation that represents a dramatic abuse of power by the older sibling. Children in such families must realize the boundaries of acceptable sexual behavior, in a way that is analogous to the boundaries of aggressive behavior in particular and emotional behavior in general.

Parents should accept allegations of sibling incest as honest declarations of genuine occurrences that must be taken seriously and acted on immediately. Parents should be fully informed about the situation from the victim (usually a daughter) and then confront the offending sibling (usually an older son) in a caring but firm fashion. In many instances, parents have their own suspicions regarding possible sexual play between the siblings and might have witnessed such play, at least to some extent. In such cases, confrontation is somewhat easier, as the question is not so much whether anything happened but precisely what happened and how often it occurred. In cases where parents have no knowledge or suspicion, the confrontation is more a case of parents trying to assess the honesty of their daughter's remarks.

Matters are made worse when their son strongly denies the accusations, accusing the younger child of spreading lies. If the son maintains this posture despite reported attempts by the parents, they might arrange a meeting at which both children are present. Since such a meeting should be conducted in a fashion sensitive to the needs of all the parties involved, it is wise to seek outside help. This type of meeting sometimes results in an agreed-upon course of events, but it rarely reveals the whole truth. Continuing to work with a professional counselor whom the family trusts to give them advice and direction and who can help them work through the disclosure process is very useful.

Most families are reluctant to reveal the matter to anyone outside the family, particularly a professional in mental or physical health, because the law requires that all sexual and physical abuse cases be reported to various state service agencies. Families fear the worst, believing that their reputations will be ruined and the family will be destroyed. The truth of the matter is that in most cases, particularly those involving sibling incest, state agencies and mental health services often work together to develop a plan aimed at appropriate treatment without recourse to criminal or legal sanctions. The worst that usually happens is that the older child might be temporarily removed from the home and placed in a foster home. Parent-child incest usually has more dramatic personal and legal consequences because the adults involved in such endeavors are supposed to be in full control of their actions, unlike nonadult siblings of younger victims.

Many types of counseling are useful in such cases. Family counseling is important to ensure more appropriate supervision of the children, as well as better communication about rules and values on the one hand and expression of feelings and events on the other. Individual counseling helps the victim work through the trauma and the perpetrator correct his or her problem. Group counseling might provide helpful peer support, advice, and criticism.

## Abuse Outside the Nuclear Family

In cases in which a child is sexually abused by someone outside the immediate family, a distinction must be made among relatives, other people with whom the child is in frequent contact, and strangers.

## Extended Family Members

Sexual abuse might occur with a cousin, uncle, aunt, grandparent, stepparent, stepsibling, and so on. Revelation of such abuse produces less strain on the nuclear family than abuse occurring within the context of the immediate family, although it still causes stress in regard to the specific relationship between the nuclear family and the person (or family) in question and to relationships throughout the entire extended family network.

Depending on how other family members perceive the validity of the accusation, the victim or perpetrator, along with his or her respective nuclear family, is usually ostracized or severely denigrated. Frequently, the family of the accused person will mobilize in defense of its vulnerable member, insinuating that the accuser is lying. This escalates into outright antagonism, with both families avoiding contact with each other and making increasingly angrier accusations and counteraccusations.

In such cases, the victim's family typically envelops the child in warmth and protectiveness, often causing the victim to regress temporarily in functioning. On the positive side, such a family tends to seek treatment for the victim, following through on therapeutic suggestions or recommendations. The alleged abuser's family typically becomes very antagonistic toward any intervention or suggested treatment, feeling that accepting such help is tantamount to a confession. In most situations, it takes strong pressure, usually from the court, for the alleged perpetrator or any member of his or her family to enter treatment. Even if the perpetrator confesses or the victim's family otherwise accepts the situation, there is often a marked strain between the families for a long time.

## Family Friends and Acquaintances

Another scenario exists between a child and a person with whom the child is familiar. The perpetrator might be an older child whom the victim knows, often through older siblings, a teacher or aide at school, a coach, a neighbor, a baby-sitter, or an adult friend. When sexual abuse involving one of these persons is reported, parents typically remove the child from contact with the person. Matters are exacerbated if the school is involved, as the school conducts its own investigation, which results in additional tension and problems. In the case of a neighbor or adult friend, families frequently confront the adult with the child's accusation. Unfortunately, such encounters are usually unproductive, as the adult in question characteristically denies any such involvement unless direct proof is provided. If the parents believe the child's story, they should communicate their findings to an outside authority, turning over the investigation to more experienced professionals. It is not helpful for parents to act as detectives or investigators, partly because they are not very objective or experienced in the matter and also because doing so will probably lead to intense encounters that might cause added problems.

In such cases, parents serve their child best by attending to his or her needs, encouraging the child to share his or her feelings and the events with a counselor, and providing greater supervision and structure in the child's life. Parents also should make some effort to prevent future occurrences by teaching all their children how to prevent sexual abuse, helping their children disclose any questionable experience they might have encountered or might encounter in the future, and in general fostering open communication about personal concerns. For the most part, nuclear family bonds are strengthened in such cases, and the family often receives support from the extended family, thereby strengthening alliances with extended family members.

### Strangers

Sexual abuse perpetrated by a stranger is very rare, but it recieves the greatest attention and elicits the most fear. This "dirty old man in the park" experience is much less common than cases in which there is great familiarity between the victim and the perpetrator, although the few cases that are reported receive undue and even exaggerated attention. This reaction is intriguing, as it represents the collective paranoia of our culture and sets up a convenient external target of blame, precisely because mutual consent or cooperation is rarely in question.

It is interesting to note, however, that as children grow older and enter mid- to late adolescence, and certainly as they enter adulthood, many cases of sexual abuse, or rape, are seen as being implicitly or explicitly provoked by the victim. Fortunately, the situation in regard to children is less complicated, as society does not consider children capable of giving fully informed consent concerning involvement in sexual matters. Some exceptions have occurred in cases of older adolescent girls who have allegedly been abused by slightly older adolescent boys, such as at a party or other social gathering. Recent investigations concerning sexual abuse of adolescent girls (both in high school and college) who were abused while intoxicated focus on the fact that abuse might have been premeditated by the perpetrator(s).

In matters of sexual abuse by strangers, families generally are extremely supportive, often mobilizing not only the immediate nuclear family and the entire extended family, but also almost all members of the community. Thus, the victimized child is typically enveloped in a network of care and protection, often to the bitter exclusion of the stranger and the group he or she represents. If the event was highly traumatic, particularly if it involved physical force or threats of violence, short-term crisis counseling might be helpful to alleviate immediate distress as well as to prevent additional agitation or future generalization.

# 9

# Victim Voices

ALL victims of sexual abuse express their emotions in some manner. This expression is usually conveyed through negative, self-destructive, and abnormal behaviors. In our experience of treating sexually abused victims, however, we have discovered that many individuals express their feelings in other, more creative ways. Some kind of expressive endeavor seems essential in cases of abuse. Allowing the child victim to be creative during the healing process provides relief from the trauma while helping the child engage in an enjoyable and stimulating activity. The resulting products also help facilitate development of coping skills (Armstrong 1978).

This chapter includes comments from victims of various ages regarding their abusive experiences, poems written by an adult survivor, and a description of specific themes that we have noticed consistently in drawings by sexually abused children. These themes also are manifested in many normal children's drawings at one time or another, but they are typically portrayed in a much more stark, intense, and obsessive fashion in drawings by sexually abused children.

## Victim Comments

He told me he loved me.

He told me not to tell anyone.

He said, "Let's keep it our special secret."

He said, "I'll hurt you and your parents."

He hurt me.

Why was I so bad?

I loved him.

He said I was only his.

He told me to suck his penis.

I hate him.

He put money down his pants.

They tied me to the bed.

I won't tell on him.

I don't want to think about it.

I don't want to see him go to jail.

I don't want to talk about it.

We played "hunt for the marble."

If I see her again, I'll kill her.

Yuck!

She said I had to obey her.

They told me sex would be fun.

He kept rubbing till it hurt.

He said I was so cute and special.

I don't know why I did it.

It was like a bad dream.

I didn't want my friends to find out.

For a while, it was worth it.

I sensed something was happening, but I couldn't figure out what.

We were like husband and wife.

I wanted him to hate me, so he would tell.

## Poems by an Adult Survivor of Incest

### *by Jo Ann Hernández*

1. *I was married to a fine man*
   *Who brought home the paycheck*
   *Never went out with the boys*
   *Was faithful and true and loyal*

   *He had his image of what I was supposed to be*
   *Wife to his house and career*
   *Mother to his children*
   *Lover to his needs*

   *I needed a protector and guardian*
   *To understand about hell*
   *To see the pain*
   *I had covered so well*

   *It was a trade-off that didn't work out*
   *It wasn't his fault or mine*
   *We had both bought the fairy-tale ending*
   *He was a prince and I was beauty*
   *With the beast inside*

   *He didn't know how my parents had fixed me*
   *So I was more beast than beauty*
   *And all his love and goodness couldn't defeat*
   *The powers within me*

   *He left confused and hurt*
   *And blaming me*
   *I taught him well*

2. *I am a bad girl*
   *because I tell family secrets*

   *I am vindictive*
   *because I make up stories*

   *I am a nuisance*
   *because I don't give up*

   *I am ungrateful*
   *because I don't appreciate them*

   *I am spiteful*
   *because I don't keep the family name honorable*

   *I am a disgrace*
   *because I lost a husband*

   *I am a failure*
   *because I lost a husband*

   *I am obnoxious*
   *because I don't shut up*

   *I am worthless*
   *because I can't have babies*

   *I am disgusting*
   *because I want the truth*

   *I am a troublemaker*
   *because I ask questions*

   *I am unforgivable*
   *because I survived them*

3. *She always said*
   *I had to buy my friends*
   *I learn well*

   *To be allowed to eat*
   *I let him do what he wanted*
   *I bought food*

   *To feel safe*
   *I kept quiet about him*
   *I bought protection*

   *To feel love*
   *I took care of them*
   *I bought affection*

   *To stay alive*
   *I let him enjoy me*
   *I bought time*

   *She said I was unlovable*
   *I had to buy my needs*
   *The price was only myself*

4.  *I saw a little girl*
    *Kiss her dad on the mouth*
    *My stomach churned*

    *I saw her lift her skirt*
    *And her father laughed*
    *I froze*

    *I saw her lay her head on his lap*
    *He stroked her hair*
    *I panicked*

    *I saw her flirt with him*
    *He smiled and threw her a kiss*
    *I ached*

    *I saw her go off to play*
    *He didn't hang on to her*
    *I cried*

    *Thank goodness is an expression*
    *That became real*
    *I was relieved*

    *Thank goodness not all dads*
    *Are like mine*

5. *I was their daughter*
*I would have settled for just being that*

*I was their mother*
*I took care of them*
*And protected them*

*I was Daddy's little girl*
*I was special and privileged*
*I took Mom's place of honor*

*I was his wife and a father to her*
*Taking sides, settling arguments*
*Making both feel good*
*And it never was enough*

*I was his lover and her competition*
*I made him feel like a man*
*She hated me and punished me*

*I was their scapegoat*
*It was my fault, my blame, my evilness*
*As long as it's me they never have to look at themselves*

*I am their truth*
*They can never forgive me for that*

6. *She said I was unlovable*
   *He would love me every night*

   *She said I was ungrateful*
   *Every night he murmured his gratitude*

   *She said I was a seducer*
   *He would never let me go*

   *She said I was evil*
   *All night long he said I was good*

   *She said I was ugly*
   *He told me I was his pretty little girl*

   *She said she was only thinking of me*
   *He would tell me he was doing it for me*

   *No one asked me*

7. *They buy me the best of foods*
*because they love me*

*They buy me the best of clothes*
*because they love me*

*They put me in the best of schools*
*because they love me*

*They beat me so I'll cry*
*because they love me*

*They use me against each other*
*because they love me*

*They call me names*
*because they love me*

*They touch me whenever and wherever*
*because they love me*

*Sometimes I wish they wouldn't love me so much*
*but then what would I be*

*People speak of moms and dads*
*as parents so dear*

*Courageous and supportive*
*A symbol to follow*

*Always there for you*
*Making you smile*

*Touching you to caress*
*Stroking your tears away*

*What did I do*
*to make mine so different?*

8. *If he wasn't so needing*
   *Would I still have to take care of him*

   *If he wasn't so big*
   *Would I be able to get away*

   *If he wasn't so violent*
   *Would I be braver*

   *If he wasn't my dad*
   *Would I be able to tell*

9. *I write better in bed*
   *Is that because*
   *All my childhood memories*
   *Come from being*
   *Flat on my back*
   *I have no memory*
   *I have no childhood*
   *Everyone talks about*
   *Lazy summer days or*
   *Games they used to play*
   *I became an old woman*
   *At the age of four*

## Drawings by Sexually Abused Children

The drawings by sexually abused children appear to revolve around one of five main themes:

1. Stark sexual images
2. Phallic symbols
3. General symbols
4. Self-image distortions
5. General confusion

### Stark Sexual Images

Such images are usually drawn in one color and consist of a series of lines. Typically, abused children draw human figures prominently displaying their genitalia. Although children who have not been abused also draw nude figures, the intensity, frequency, detail, and accompanying stories of abused children make the reason behind the drawings and the drawings themselves quite different.

### Phallic Symbols

Phallic symbols are shapes that represent the male genital organ (penis). The most repeated phallic shape depicted in the drawings of sexually abused children is that of a snake or snakelike figure. In contrast to nonabused children, sexually abused children typically verify at some point that the snake is a penis and might actually name the snake after the perpetrator and recount the traumatic incident.

### General Symbols

Signs and emblems have been used throughout history to depict specific objects or situations. The dove is a symbol of peace, the eagle a symbol of power, water a symbol of rebirth, and so on. The symbols and emblems repeatedly drawn by sexually abused children are those of broken hearts, rainbows, spirals, wheels, rain, and black skies. Unlike the first two types of drawings, these are of a much more general nature and are typically revealing of a more generalized distress rather than sexual abuse as such. For instance, familiar drawings in the wake of adolescent breakups are of broken hearts, cloudy scenes, and dark skies. Similar themes are manifested in drawings made by people who are depressed. If a child makes these kinds of drawings, they should be viewed as a sign of emotional distress—for instance, a bad mood brought on by melancholy thinking—not necessarily as a sign of a deep trauma or of sexual abuse. If a child repeatedly creates these drawings, however, it is likely that he or she is experiencing an emotional problem that requires some attention. Only further discussion of an open and accepting nature will reveal whether the disturbance is related to sexual abuse.

### Self-image Distortions

In children's drawings of themselves, mental images of the self are transferred to paper, often in a very revealing and largely unconscious manner. The trauma of sexual abuse definitely affects a child's self-image. Typically, this type of drawing depicts a child who is small in size and distorted in one or more ways. These distortions often involve the body parts affected by the abuse. For example, a girl who was forced to have oral sex might draw a picture of herself with a huge mouth. It is important never to analyze a child's drawing as indicative of abuse without talking to the child first and seeking help from a mental health professional trained in interpreting drawings.

### General Confusion

Most sexually abused children experience their lives as a state of chaos. It is often difficult for them to attain harmony, security, and strength because of the constant fear they experience. The repeated visual signs of confusion we have observed in drawings of sexually abused children are densely overlapping scribbles, circles, or ovals. Again, it is important not to confuse this kind of scribbling with the early scribbles made by toddlers. Scribbles suggesting sexual abuse are those made by older children who have long passed the toddler stage but who regress in their drawings, and usually their behavior. Moreover, such children will often confess that they are confused and distressed.

Remember not to interpret pictures as signs of sexual abuse without consulting a professional, as all the above-mentioned categories are observed in children who have not been abused. Only repeated images of singular intensity that are drawn in obsessive and compulsive ways are of genuine concern. If a child repeatedly draws any of the above themes, ask her or him to tell you about the pictures. If you are still concerned after the discussion, it is advisable to seek professional advice to help you assess the type of stress the child might be experiencing.

# 10

# The Perpetrator

U P to this point, we have focused primarily on the victim of sexual abuse. But every abuse situation has another side, involving one or more perpetrators who have abused one or more children. This chapter examines the sex offender's characteristics in more detail, sorting out the diverse myths and generalizations that have arisen concerning the offender.

## The Stereotype

Over the years, many myths about the "typical" child molester have developed. The picture is one of a dirty old man, wearing a trench coat and lurking in alleys, parks, or school yards, poised to attack his prey. This man often has distorted features, such as scars and facial abnormalities, an alcohol or drug addiction, and mental or emotional problems. If boys are victimized, the man is considered to be a homosexual.

Occasionally, this image is modified to portray a pathetic and vulnerable man manipulated by seductive children into engaging in sexual abuse. Naturally, this position is taken by many perpetrators themselves, especially those who deny any responsibility for their actions or refuse to recognize that the abuse was in any way wrong or problematic. Even if they do admit their involvement, they usually blame the victim: "Girls who dress sexy are asking for it" or "Women have a secret desire to be raped and usually enjoy it."

## The Reality

A sex offender or perpetrator, also known as a child molester, is usually significantly older than the victim. Although offenders can be male or female, the majority of offenders are male, with estimates ranging from 80 to 98 percent (Russell 1986). Other characteristics include the following:

Most sex offenders know their victim, at least minimally.

Close to 50 percent of sex offenders interviewed admitted to committing their first sexual offense before the age of eighteen (Groth 1979).

Alcohol or drug use, insanity, retardation, and homosexuality are *not* significant characteristics of offenders.

Sex offenders are concerned mainly with meeting their own needs.

Sex offenders characteristically commit their offenses alone.

Sex offenders see themselves as helpless victims of controlling and powerful environments.

Sex offenders are emotionally immature, having little understanding of their own behavior.

Most sex offenders have poor impulse control, low self-esteem, poor communication skills, and poor socialization skills.

The vast majority of sex offenders were previous victims of sexual or physical abuse. Although precise estimates vary, studies show that childhood abuse is five to ten times more prevalent in sex offenders than in control groups.

Sex offenders who molest very young children (pedophiles) molest, on the average, 150 children before they are caught, about 380 children during the course of the offenders' lives (Freeman-Longo 1985).

The vast majority (more than 75 percent) of incest offenders also abuse children outside the family (Russell 1986).

## Characteristics

There are two main types of sex offenders, regressed and fixated. *Regressed offenders* are people who have shown a capacity to form appropriate peer relationships and sexual attachments but tend to regress to a more primitive mode of functioning following stresses of various kinds. *Fixated offenders* never attain such normalcy in relationships and always remain attracted to children; they are thus fixated at an earlier developmental stage.

Fixated offenders are often divided into two subgroups, *pedophiles* and *hebephiles*, depending on whether their sexual attraction is toward prepubescent or pubescent children, respectively. Incest and pedophilia are not the same. *Incest* refers to sexual involvement with a relative, while *pedophilia* refers to sexual attraction to prepubescent children. These can overlap, however, if the prepubescent child becomes a victim of his or her parent.

Different emotional patterns are also evident, chronic obsessive and acute regressive. The *chronic obsessive* pattern is most apparent in pedophiles and is characterized by constant thinking, fantasizing, and ruminating about children and adolescents in general or a specific child or adolescent in particular. This person's life is dominated by his or her obsession. The person finds adult sexual or peer relationships repulsive because of the overwhelming fear of rejection and inadequacy. This fixated sexual preference for children usually begins when the offender is an adolescent and continues throughout his or her life. Typically, obsessive offenders do not experience much guilt or shame about their sexual behavior, as they strongly need, value and want relationships with children. Frequently, they are even intellectually and emotionally convinced of the merits of such relationships.

*Acute regressive* offenders tend to react to stressful situations in acute ways. Thus, the sex offender acts impulsively because his or her adult sexual channels are too stressful or upsetting. The offender becomes desperate, replacing the adult partner with a child in order to gain sexual gratification. After the offense is committed, the depressed offender feels inadequate, remorseful, disgusted, and guilty. These feelings arise only after the sexual offense has occurred, however.

In summary, the obsessive offender's behavior is chronic and the sexual offense premeditated. The sexual preference of this type of offender is always a child or adolescent. The regressive offender's behavior is acute, and the sexual offense occurs impulsively. This type of offender typically prefers to have a sexual relationship with an adult peer until a conflict occurs, at which time the offender turns to children for sexual gratification.

## Types of Sexual Assault

Child sexual assault can be categorized into four types: pressured sexual assault, forced sexual assault, sadistic sexual assault, and noncontact offenses of various kinds.

### Pressured Sexual Assault

In this type of offense, there is a lack of physical force. Rather, the offender entices the child victim by using persuasion. The offender does this either by bribing the child with money, gifts, outings, or treats or by rewarding the child with affection or attention. At some level, the offender genuinely desires and cares about the child and looks at him or her as a loving, undemanding, open, affectionate, but essentially powerless person. Aspects of aggression are present, but they are typically suppressed. The offender feels quite safe with the child and very often knows the child prior to any sexual involvement. This type of sexual attraction and involvement might continue over an extended period of time. Sexual acts carried out tend to be somewhat normal (for appropriate partners) and are often conducted in pseudoaffectionate ways.

### Forced Sexual Assault

A second type of sexual offense is characterized by the use of physical harm or threats. The offender physically threatens, attacks, and overpowers the child by means of intimidation with threats of harm or with the use of a weapon or occasionally physical force. The offender usually has no intention of hurting the victim and only uses whatever force is necessary to satisfy his or her sexual needs. The child is seen as a temporary sexual object, so continued sexual involvement is minimal. The offender views the child victim as weak, helpless, and easily manipulated. The offender, in turn, feels strong and in charge. This type of offender usually will not accept no for an answer and will use whatever means it takes to overpower the victim. The general atmosphere is one of pressure and control, with sexual acts frequently consisting of oral as well as genital sex.

### Sadistic Sexual Assault

Another type of sexual offense is characterized by the desire to hurt or punish the child victim in some way. In order to become sexually excited, the offender tends to inflict pain, either through brute force or with the use of a weapon (such as a knife, gun, rope, chain, or pipe). Sexual behaviors themselves are often highly deviant or perverted; anal sex and rape are common. This type of assault is planned for some time, and thus is premeditated. Much primitive rage is present in these cases. Occasionally, this reaches extreme proportions in episodes of gang rape wherein a multitude of offenders rapes a solitary victim.

### Noncontact Offenses

The last type of offense includes a variety of abuse and misuse behaviors that do not involve direct physical contact, including voyeurism, exposure to or participation in pornography, and exhibitionism. Most offenders in this category are highly passive individuals who have great trouble expressing their anger, establishing viable peer relationships, and generally fitting into society. They get aroused by shocking or manipulating weaker or more ignorant people. As children typically possess both these attributes, the offenders commonly gravitate toward them. They do not desire any direct relationship with the victim, tending to choose a stranger whenever possible and to have short-term contact with the victim. Sexual feelings generated in the offender typically are accompanied by masturbation during or after the abusive incident. Victims sometimes experience vague anxiety or fear but are often more confused, surprised, shocked, and even emotionally or sexually excited. Victims also experience more general feelings of being manipulated or exploited.

## Adolescent Sex Offenders

Sexual offenders are commonly believed to be adult males, but in recent years an increased number of sexual offenses committed by juveniles has been reported. National crime reports indicate that between 20 and 30 percent of sex offenses are committed by offenders under eighteen years of age. Several research studies suggest that over 50 percent of adult sex offenders began their sexual deviancy during their adolescent years (Freeman-Longo 1985). Several cases have involved children under age ten. Despite the growing number of sexual assaults committed by adolescents, there is significant reluctance to view juvenile sexual assaults as serious. Most parents and some professionals feel that intervention and treatment will stigmatize the adolescent for life and instead believe that "getting on with things" is the best approach. As such, adolescents rarely receive specialized treatment to prevent them from committing future sexual assaults. It seems clear, however, that if adolescent sex offenders are not apprehended and do not receive treatment, they are at an extremely high risk to victimize others, especially younger children. It is of crucial importance for any adolescent who commits a sexual offense to be apprehended and receive specialized treatment.

Adolescent offenders and their related offenses share certain general characteristics (Freeman-Longo 1985):

Most adolescent sex offenders were sexually victimized as children, perceive an early childhood experience as sexual victimization, or psychosexually experience their own sexuality in a maladaptive and socially unacceptable way.

Adolescent sex offenders use sexual victimization of others to reduce or eliminate feelings of anxiety, especially regarding interpersonal skills or relationships. This anxiety stems from feeling out of control, helpless, incompetent, powerless, fearful, inferior, or totally inadequate.

Sexual victimization of others is *not* an impulsive act, especially if it is an act of rape. The act is typically premeditated, although the timing of the offense and the choice of the victim might be impulsive.

Prior to acting out the sexual assault, the troubled adolescent usually has generated several assault fantasies to reduce feelings of anxiety. These fantasies gradually become more violent in nature until the adolescent actually commits an offense.

Prior to rape, the adolescent has typically committed some other type of sexual assault. This might include voyeurism, exhibitionism, stalking a potential victim, grabbing and touching the private body parts of a potential victim, or masturbating to fantasies about a specific individual.

Adolescent sex offenders frequently experience and display anger. Anger is almost too accessible to them and frequently precipitates the actual offense.

Adolescent sex offenders have rigid value systems. They perceive things in black and white, thinking, for example, that sex is bad, all women are prostitutes, or people should be exploited before they exploit you.

Adolescent sex offenders have limited knowledge of appropriate social interactions, along with poorly developed social skills.

Adolescent sex offenders depersonalize the potential victim in order to seek dominance and power over him or her.

Adolescent sex offenders fall into two distinct categories, nonaggressive and aggressive. *Nonaggressive* sex offenders employ little or no force during the offense, tending to use more subtle and manipulative means of coercion, such as bribery, trickery, sarcasm, or goading.

They are typically isolated youths, estranged from warm peer and family relationships; they have few or no close friends. They have very low self-esteem and are often deeply depressed, experiencing their lives as failures. They often appear on the surface to be relatively well adjusted and rarely display behavioral or substance abuse problems before, during, or after the abusive incidents. School performance is, however, often negatively affected. Thus, the nonaggressive adolescent sex offender is shy, withdrawn, and of average or below average intelligence. He or she engages in sexual activity with younger children, tending to prefer those in early childhood (three to six years old). Baby-sitting is a common environment in which this type of abuse occurs. Actual abuse can range from solitary episodes of sexual experimentation, voyeurism, or exhibitionism to more chronic sexual compulsions. All episodes are of a non-forceful nature and can be seen as pathetic and distorted ways of attempting to gain intimacy and acceptance.

*Aggressive* sex offenders use force or violence, employing direct methods of coercion, frequently with a weapon or overt display of power. They are typically intensely involved with a peer group, often as one of the more active or powerful members. They usually have a girlfriend or boyfriend, a part-time job, and an active social life. Such offenders often have a prior history of antisocial behavior and are likely to have abused alcohol or drugs. Boys represent the vast majority of this group. Thus, the aggressive sex offender is typically loud, obnoxious, and intelligent. He or she tends to seek out victims in the latency or preadolescent stage (six through fifteen years old). Such male offenders frequently have committed rape, often of their girlfriends. The abusive episodes can be viewed as exercises of power, control, or egocentric need gratification.

Both these types of adolescent sex offenders are treatable if they are apprehended early and specialized treatment is mandated. It is important for parents and teachers to accept the fact that the adolescent has committed a sexual offense, to display a strong conviction that what happened was wrong and that it was the adolescent's fault, and to support him or her in dealing with the problem. It is also helpful to ask the adolescent about his or her own abuse, assuming that there is a strong likelihood that such abuse has occurred. Instead of simply asking whether the adolescent was abused in the past, ask how the prior abuse occurred. After these personal discussions, it is important to seek treatment for the adolescent from someone who has worked with sex offenders and will address the particular sexual abuse dynamics involved. Both groups and individual treatment approaches appear to be helpful, the former to confront resistance by offering direct feedback from peers and the latter to work through underlying emotional issues.

The general goals of therapy are as follows:

1. To break down the denial system
2. To help the adolescent fully disclose the nature, content, and fantasies involved in the abuse
3. To determine the specific behavioral and sexual arousal systems involved and to provide more appropriate alternatives
4. To assess and work through other unresolved emotional issues
5. To evaluate family factors, strengths, and dynamics and to intervene accordingly in the family system
6. To help with social and interpersonal skill deficits
7. To assist in planning for successful reentry into the family, school, and community.

Some adolescents need specialized treatment because of the type of sexual offense committed. If no facility offering such treatment is located nearby, find out where such treatment can be obtained. In any case, the adolescent must receive specialized treatment if he or she has any chance of learning how to stop sexually victimizing others.

# 11

# The Legal Process

I F you are convinced, even reasonably so, that a child is telling the truth about an abusive situation, you should contact the state social services division that deals with cases of abuse and neglect. If you do not know whom to contact, call a professional who specializes in children's services, such as a pediatrician, guidance counselor, school principal, child therapist, or any state or community agency providing services to children. Most states are required to act within one to three days, typically by sending out a trained caseworker to investigate matters. Frequently, the caseworker is accompanied by a police officer or someone selected by the state attorney's office, since this is also a potential criminal offense.

These people interview the child separately (typically in a context other than that in which the abuse was reported to have occurred), interview the parents either separately or together (depending on the case), and interview the perpetrator (sometimes at a later time). If, after discussing the case between themselves and with their supervisors, the investigators believe that the child has been sexually abused, immediate steps will be taken to guarantee the security of the child, particularly by decreasing or eliminating contact between the child and the alleged perpetrator. In an incest case, this usually means physical removal of one or the other family member (ideally, the perpetrator) from the home via a restraining order and, if necessary, police action.

Plans are then made to conduct more extensive evaluations of all relevant parties, as well as to obtain treatment for the child victim and perhaps the perpetrator. Meanwhile, the criminal justice division gathers information and decides whether to press charges based on the exact nature of the case and the quantity and quality of incriminating evidence. Evidence is typically obtained as if the case will be taken to court (Burgess et al. 1978). The social services division of a state or community typically assesses the family setting in a more comprehensive manner, possibly providing specific therapeutic services.

If charges will be brought against the perpetrator, a forensic evaluation of all parties often is requested. This provides a fairly neutral and systematic evaluation of the many facets of the case. Direct evidence and testimony from each family member, as well as from any other person who has important information or is connected in some way to the case, is routinely solicited.

States vary in how they handle a child victim's testimony, sometimes asking the child to testify openly in court or in closed chambers, reviewing videotaped sessions conducted in advance, or hearing relevant testimony from an evaluator, therapist, or court-appointed advocate. Although legal representatives try to make the experience as stress-free as possible for the child, court appearances are emotionally draining and very difficult for anyone, especially children. Many states are working on specific strategies to help reduce stress, including accepting videotaped testimony or observations noted from behind a one-way mirror as evidence in the courtroom, while trying to maintain the right of the accused to confront the accuser face to face. This is not a simple matter, however, as the often conflicting needs and rights of victims and accused have inspired much legal controversy.

## The Interview

One of the most traumatic events the child might experience is recounting the assault. To minimize this trauma, it is important that you, as the child's parent, teacher, or advocate, insist that all mandated parties be present for the interview. These parties should include trained representatives from the police, state attorney's office, social service agency, and mental health agency. In addition, a medical professional should be consulted if the child is physically hurt or is in need of medical attention.

It should be noted that most states employ personnel trained in interviewing children who have been sexually abused. Inquire before the interview whether the professionals speaking to your child have had specific training in sexual abuse. If they do not, insist that someone with the proper training interview the child. Parents should insist on speaking with the interviewer prior to the interviewer's meeting with the child. This allows them to put their minds at ease and clarify any questions about the proceedings. Here are some questions a parent or teacher might want to ask:

Where will the interview take place?

Out of all mandated persons attending, who will be doing the interviewing?

What will be the specific seating arrangement?

What techniques and questions will the interviewer use?

How long will the interview take?

When will I (the parent or teacher) be given information about what will happen after the interview?

During the interviewing process, it is important that the parents' reactions be supportive, calm, and reassuring to the child. Just as the retelling of the assault is traumatizing to the child, so will be the negative or overly emotional reactions of the parents. If needed, parents should avail themselves of support throughout the crisis from medical, religious, or mental health professionals. If a parent is overly distressed, it is beneficial to ask someone else to be with the child during the interview. A guardian *ad litem* or child advocate also might be appointed for this purpose.

The interviewing process should take place in a pleasing and calm location free from any distractions. The home might be a suitable site, as long as the assault did not take place there. The school often provides a more neutral and less intrusive setting. In any case, the child's emotional well-being should be the most important criterion.

The timing of the interview is crucial in obtaining the most accurate and descriptive information. It is important that it take place as soon as possible after the assault has been reported, especially if it involves incest or a situation in which the offender might have ongoing contact with the victim.

Interviewing techniques differ from case to case, but because children often find it difficult to verbalize emotional situations, more action-oriented strategies are usually used. Thus, interviewers might use anatomically correct dolls, pictures, books, and drawing materials, depending on the assessed maturity and capabilities of the child. Interviewers often ask the child to discuss, draw, or act out "the worst thing that ever happened to you," "the worst thing that happened to your body," or "the worst thing that an adult has done to you (or your body)."

Besides compiling information about what happened, the interviewer also must assess whether the child is credible and can describe events consistently in regard to time and detail. The age of the child is an important factor in determining whether the exact chronology of events and specific details concerning the abuse can be pinpointed.

In ending the interview, the same calm, supportive approach is required. Ending the interview hastily could be traumatic for the child. The interviewer should ask whether he or she has any questions; if so, the interviewer should provide clear, direct, and honest answers appropriate to the child's level of understanding.

## Determination of Prosecution

After the interview has taken place, the police investigator writes a report. This report is given to the state attorney or prosecutor, who then reads the information and decides whether an arrest should be made. How this decision is made depends on the facts discovered in the police investigation. If the state attorney believes that a crime has been committed, an arrest is made (Goldstein 1987). Whenever possible, sexual abuse cases are prosecuted.

The arrest affidavit includes a brief description of the offense, a summary of the police investigator's actions, pertinent medical information, statements from the victim and any witnesses, evidence found by the police investigator, and the specific charges against the offender. After the arrest affidavit is prepared and notarized, it is sent to the court for a judge to review. If the judge believes that a sexual offense has been committed beyond a reasonable doubt, a warrant for the arrest of the offender is issued. This process takes anywhere from one day to several weeks. Immediate action is not always possible, unless the abuse was distinctly flagrant or violent or the offender is a clear danger to other people. Once again, it is helpful for parents or teachers to find sources of support from relevant professionals if they feel too distressed during this process.

If an arrest is made, the court might set a bond. This decision is made either by a judge or the police. Whether a bond is set is determined by several factors, including whether the offender is likely to appear in court when the case is presented, whether the offender has committed any previous crimes, and whether signing a written promise to appear in court will be sufficient.

Throughout this process, it is important to remember that the perpetrator has legal rights in the matter and should not be prematurely condemned. Furthermore, since all people are considered innocent until proven guilty, matters often proceed slowly in an effort to make sure the rights of all parties are being protected.

If no bond is set and you fear that the child will be in jeopardy, you might want to file for a restraining order that would limit or stop all contact between the child and the offender until the case is heard in court. Enforcing a restraining order is often difficult because an adult must supervise the child at all times and call the police if the offender appears. It does provide some protection for the child, however.

One disappointing event that can occur regarding prosecution, is when an offense has occurred but the prosecutor cannot press charges because of lack of evidence, unavailability of witnesses, an incomplete police investigation, violation of the offender's rights, or an inability to get concrete testimony (for example, if the victim is unable to testify because of age or a handicapping condition). In this case, a parent or guardian is forced to take charge of the situation, providing some measure of protection from the suspected offender, reassurance that the child is believed and not at fault, and therapeutic assistance to help the child work through related emotional, behavioral, and learning problems.

## The Child's Deposition

A deposition is the testimony of a witness under oath often used in lieu of court appearance. A deposition will be taken of everyone who was involved in the alleged abuse or has information relevant to the case. This might include the victim, the offender, witnesses, the therapist, the caseworker, parents, relatives, teacher(s), a guidance counselor, friends, and so on.

During the deposition, the child answers questions regarding the offense under oath before the judicial recorder. At first the questions are general: "What is your name?" "Where do you live?" "Do you know what a lie is?" Specific questions follow: "What happened?" "Who did it?" "Where did it happen?" "How often?" "Was anyone else present?" Often the defense attorney repeats these questions to see whether the child gives consistent responses. The attorney also asks questions in different ways to get the full story and identify any inconsistencies or contradictions. All of this might upset the child greatly, causing much anxiety and sometimes emotional distress. You can help the child through this by being supportive, having the child's lawyer stop the questioning until the child calms down, and insisting that the questions be clear, direct, and relevant.

Besides the parent, child, child's attorney, and defense attorney, a court reporter will be present to record everything that is said. If the attorney who is questioning the child asks something that the child did not understand or did not hear, the court reporter can review the record and repeat the question. The report is subsequently typed up and made available to the relevant authorities, as well as to the child's parents or legal guardians. The deposition can be taken at the state attorney's office or at the office of the child's therapist. All steps to ensure optimum comfort and familiarity should be taken, although the setting should be neutral and professional. Taking the deposition might last anywhere from a half hour to three hours, depending on the nature of the offense and the circumstances of the case.

Taking a deposition is a necessary but difficult part of the court process. It should not, however, revictimize the child in any way.

## Forensic Evaluations

A forensic evaluation is conducted by mental health professionals and is accepted as evidence by a court of law. Unlike other contact with mental health professionals, the specific contents and results of this evaluation are *not* confidential. Rather, all relevant information is reported. The report includes documentation regarding the child's intelligence, behavior, credibility, mental status, and family history. Offenders also can be the subject of forensic evaluations.

These evaluations are quite comprehensive, addressing many areas of functioning. The child is evaluated by one or two professionals (preferably a man and a woman) skilled in forensic matters in general and sexual abuse cases in particular. This evaluation consists of both formal and informal tests, assessing cognitive, behavioral, and personality characteristics. In addition to the child, other people are often interviewed, including parents, teachers, and any other sources of information. In incest cases, the alleged offender often is evaluated, with particular care and scrutiny being given to the specific interaction between the alleged victim and offender. More comprehensive forensic evaluations examine interactional dynamics in various systems and subsystems, especially those within the family or the context in which the abuse was reported to have occurred.

After the forensic evaluation is completed, the evaluators examine and review the data, then write a formal report consisting of findings and recommendations. This document is sent to the appropriate authorities in the legal or social service professions, and may be presented as evidence during a court trial. The evaluator(s) may be subpoenaed if necessary to discuss the information, conclusions, and recommendations contained in the report. If the case does go to court, the forensic evaluation will be an important document in conjunction with the initial interview and deposition.

Because the evaluator is regarded as an expert witness by the state and typically has extensive qualifications and experience working with sexually abused children, the child should not be too distressed by the process. Indeed, the child might be anxious and apprehensive, but if general procedures regarding the evaluation are described beforehand, the experience should not be overly upsetting.

## Court Proceedings

In recent years, some progress has been made in reducing the stress a child experiences as a result of the court process, especially in regard to testimony and cross-examination. For example, an increasing number of states allow admission of videotaped interviews of the child conducted by a therapist (with both lawyers present) in lieu of direct testimony. They also allow the presence of an advocate who accompanies the child to court and advises the judge of the child's needs. Furthermore, courts of family law are being established with more highly trained people who are aware of domestic problems of various kinds, including physical and sexual abuse, divorce, and family violence.

Alleged offenders also have certain rights, however, among which are the right to a fair and public trial and the right to confront their accuser through cross-examination. Because of these rights, children are sometimes required to appear in court. This happens most frequently in cases where concrete outside evidence is scarce or nonexistent, when the child is older (especially in adolescence), when no witnesses are available, or when the child's credibility is questionable. In such cases, the child will be served a subpoena, a document that is issued by the court to a law enforcement officer who in turn hand-delivers it to the appropriate person. Included in the document is the mandate to appear in court, the location of the court hearing, the date and time of appearance, the type of testimony, and the source of the request.

It is extremely important that children be carefully prepared before going to court. Preparation helps relax the child by making the situation more understandable and less frightening. It should include honest and complete discussion, active role playing and modeling of specific procedures that will be followed, and suggested methods of responding to questions. Naturally, the content of the child's testimony should not be altered in any substantial way during this preparation, as doing so will only hurt the child's case in the long run. Recommended stress-reducing activities include the following:

Familiarize the child with criminal justice procedures.

Familiarize the child with the courtroom.

Familiarize the child with cross-examination and related techniques.

Role-play exactly what will take place at the hearing.

Tell the child what he or she can do if questioning becomes stressful. This might include taking a break, asking for the question to be repeated in a different way, or looking only at the lawyer or judge.

Help the child tell the story in a simple and direct manner.

In conjunction with the child's lawyer or advocate, review with the child any other courtroom procedures.

A court appearance might not be necessary if the offender pleads guilty. Many courts allow videotaped interviews of the child prior to the hearing if the offender pleads guilty or if the child is too young to provide verbal or concrete testimony.

The child might have a guardian *ad litem* or child advocate appointed by the court. The role of this person is to protect and represent the child's best interest. He or she is an impartial, sensitive, and informed professional who will work directly with the child and is often very helpful throughout the court process. If a child advocate is not appointed, a lawyer, caseworker, counselor, or therapist often can provide helpful assistance and preparation during the court ordeal.

Although the above descriptions pertain to victims, precisely the same procedure can be followed when the child is an alleged offender. In that event, forensic evaluations are equally important to assess issues of credibility, abilities, and dynamics. In addition, such evaluations are sometimes useful in breaking through an offender's denial system and opening him or her up to outside help. It is important to support the alleged offender in a fundamental way, while making clear that the abuse is intolerable and must stop. Offenders should be assisted and supported in making full disclosures so that they and their victims can successfully work through their problems. An admission of guilt also helps the victim, as it reduces the victim's feeling of responsibility for the abuse or the consequences stemming from it. It also represents the first step toward being able to form a trusting relationship, a possibility previously impossible due to the abuse and the secrecy surrounding it. Even if the offender admits his or her guilt, however, formal prosecution often takes place. This appears to be crucial in maintaining supervision, control, and compliance with treatment even when imprisonment is not recommended.

## Publicity

Initial reports to state agencies are treated confidentially, but if a case is slated for criminal prosecution, such information is available to the public and is commonly reported in the news media. In addition, investigations by professionals and the associated stress in the family are often noticed by others or revealed by family members. In either case, other people become aware of the charges, as well as of various (usually incomplete) details of the case. These often have social repercussions, which constitute another source of stress for all involved, particularly the child victim, the perpetrator, and the family as a whole. The child is often viewed with a mixed sense of pity and withdrawal, the perpetrator with a strong sense of anger and disgust, and the family with varying emotions (more positive sympathy if the abuser was an outsider, more alienation and stigmatization if incest occurred). The child is seen as tainted and the perpetrator as an animal. Eventually, all those involved are shunned, the child and family in subtle psychological ways and the perpetrator in more direct and active ways. Occasionally, the perpetrator is forced to leave his or her job and the child must withdraw from school because of actual or perceived criticism.

News reports also can affect cases dramatically, so the media should take care not to identify the child by name or implication. Offenders waive the right to confidentiality by being accused and prosecuted, although some have sued for libel in cases where they were found innocent.

Publicity must be handled openly and honestly with children. They must realize that others will respond to them in ways different from before but that things will settle down after a while. Children also must be constantly assured that they did the right thing by disclosing the secret of the sexual abuse. In the wake of adverse social criticism and gossip, growing feelings of guilt and sympathy, tension at home, and hassles regarding legal matters, they frequently wish they had never disclosed the abuse. Children also need help in addressing directed social criticism stemming from the abuse. As such, they can be coached to do the following:

Ignore such remarks.

Clarify misconceptions in a rational way.

Assertively express feelings of irritation and work toward mutual understanding.

Isolate the most critical attackers and attempt to work through problems on a one-to-one basis.

Use sources of support in coping with the various stresses and securing advice.

# 12

# Morals and Boundaries: The Dynamics of Sexual Abuse

P ERHAPS the questions parents most often ask are "How can this kind of thing happen?" and "Why do people do such things?" Although these are extremely important questions, there are no clear answers. Just as in the case of crime in general, people engage in wrongful and illegal actions for various reasons. Despite this diversity, however, there do appear to be several critical factors associated with sexual abuse. These do not provide a complete explanation of why sexual abuse is perpetrated by a certain person or against a given victim, but they do describe the typically complex dynamics involved in such cases. Following is a description of these major factors, along with speculations about how they might influence or precipitate sexual abuse.

## Perpetrator Problems

By far the most important indicator of future abuse for both perpetrator and victim is a history of prior victimization. It has been reported that about 80 percent of perpetrators were abused as children or adolescents (Freeman-Longo 1985). What accounts for this phenomenally high percentage? The answers are complex, but they seem to involve a combination of modeling, reenactment of the traumatic situation(s), displacement of emotional arousal, quest for power and control, excessive sexual curiosity (inspired by premature exposure to sexuality), and a learned response to gain affection and nurturance.

The repetition and reenactment of the sexual trauma seems to be the most vicious legacy of sexual abuse: *Abuse fosters abuse.* In case after case, perpetrators reveal detailed histories of being sexually abused, often in highly traumatic ways. Characteristically, these incidents were never revealed, confessed, or worked through. Most of the abusers of such perpetrators remained unpunished and even undiscovered. The negative emotions engendered by the abuse fester within the victim, causing emotional and behavioral problems of major proportions. Eventually, the cycle repeats itself, with the past victim now victimizing someone else.

Thus, perpetrators often exhibit signs of significant emotional and behavioral disturbance. They frequently have problems in dealing with adults (especially of the opposite sex) and have underdeveloped social skills. They are drawn to children in part because of their ability to control them and exercise power over them. As such, they can successfully manipulate a more vulnerable person to engage in actions that satisfy the perpetrator's punitive desires for power, affection, and pleasure.

## Lack of Inhibitions

Frequently, sexual abuse cases occur in part because of glaring deficiencies in supervision, along with disinhibiting agents affecting the perpetrator and occasionally the victim as well. Protective parent figures are often either absent or blind to the matter, having little sense of the child's feelings or behaviors, and are not able to communicate effectively with the child. Perpetrators are typically in a highly emotional state, often acting impulsively due to external agents such as alcohol or drugs. At times, other pathological conditions might be present, including psychosis, impulse control disorder, senility, or pedophilia.

Another indirect source of a lack of inhibition is the relatively lax (until recently) safeguards, precautions, and penalties concerning sexual abuse. Not until the second half of the twentieth century has incest been considered a major crime.

## Victim Vulnerability

Sexual abuse victims are often in highly vulnerable positions. As children, they have little direct power in society. When confronted by an apparently caring and rational adult who tells them that sexual play is both acceptable and desirable, children find it difficult to refuse, having been conditioned to obey older people.

In addition, some older children are emotionally insecure or immature and as such are less likely to resist abusive encounters. In addition, many children are not knowledgeable about sexual matters and thus have little or no inclination that what they are doing is wrong. Even if they suspect that something is not right, they are told in seductive or aggressive ways that they should keep the special secret and not tell others. Previous victims of sexual abuse, especially girls, are particularly vulnerable to being abused again.

## Social Changes

Social changes in this century have affected the nature of interpersonal relationships, as well as moral values associated with love, affection, and sexuality. Although there are no clear cause-and-effect relationships, human behavior in the 1980s, particularly with respect to sexuality and interpersonal relationships, is markedly different from human behavior as recently as the last generation. There has been an increasing liberalization of attitudes concerning premarital sex, homosexuality, divorce, multiple marriages, adoption, stepfamilies, cohabitation (unmarried couples living together), and depiction of explicit sex and aggression in magazines and movies. Moreover, the status and power of women has grown significantly in this century, particularly during the past two decades, allowing for more personal and financial independence of women in respect to men. These changes have made sexuality both more titillating and more complicated.

Perhaps the most difficult transition has been the one men have had to make in regard to the liberation of women. No longer is there a clear and consistent religious or cultural message concerning sexuality and male-female relationships. Although some men have been able to adapt to the more independent and sexually liberated role of women in society, others have not. The latter group can be divided into two subgroups. Men in the first subgroup have maintained their rigidly masculine ways of looking at the world, sometimes finding a female mate who agrees with their point of view but more often floundering in relationships. Men in the second subgroup have been unable or unwilling to sustain any involvement with women, turning instead to hobbies, work, social groups and clubs, other men, children, pornography, prostitutes, or exotic adventures to substitute for the absence of a female counterpart. It is from this subgroup that many perpetrators of child sexual abuse come.

Perhaps involvement with children recreates the traditional way men treated women. It is no coincidence that women and children have been often lumped together in terms of dependency and lack of power. Thus, men who are unable to view adult women as equals in power and control turn to children, which allows them to assert their perceived masculinity by exercising power, force, and persuasion over an easily manipulated, often female, victim.

The dynamics of female perpetrators are less clear, although they also appear to use children to overcome their own feelings of powerlessness and rejection. In either case, children have become the sexual objects of maladjusted adults who are unable to deal with the pressures of modern society.

## Marital and Family Factors

These factors seem to be particularly important in cases of incest but are relevant to most sexual abuse cases. Families have undergone marked changes in this century, changes that have greatly affected their viability, consistency, and stability. It is estimated that close to 50 percent of new marriages will end in divorce, that most children will spend a significant period of time living with only one adult, that stepfamilies will outnumber traditional nuclear families in the near future, and that links with extended families will become even more fragmented and disjointed (L'Abate 1985).

These dramatic changes have had a big impact on family functioning, blurring traditional role boundaries and creating a whole new network of relationships with half siblings and steprelatives. These relationships are ill-defined by American culture, resulting in significant domestic confusion. Rules concerning physical contact and affection in stepfamilies are especially confusing. This, along with the overall liberalization of sexual behavior, has clouded the issue of incest, making the taboo against incest less intense in reconstituted families than in natural families. These boundaries typically remain intact in most reconstituted families, but there is more confusion about the precise nature of the various interpersonal relationships that exist in the new family organization. These boundaries are truly tested only in times of stress, particularly stress during a marriage or divorce. At such times, the boundaries frequently are not strong enough to sustain the pressures on them. It is frequently observed, for example, that incest typically highlights a major problem in the parents' marriage, a problem with which one of the parents copes by taking a substitute mate in the form of a child.

In general, these myriad family changes, especially when viewed in conjunction with the aforementioned social factors concerning changes in the roles of men and women, have caused increasing confusion in almost all families. Undeniably, incest is a universal phenomenon that is as old as the human race, a fact that is attested to by countless examples and by the intensity and universality of the incest taboo itself. But the recent changes in families must be considered as forces that are eroding the social and personal inhibitions concerning incest. Moreover, these changes affect family members' relationships with people outside the family, for along with the increasing latitude allowed in relationships, the growing instability and confusion within families hampers the development of clearly articulated moral guidelines in respect to love, sexuality, and power. It is thus not surprising that incest rates are about four to seven times higher in stepfamilies than in natural families (Russell 1986).

## Children's Special Allure

Over the last three centuries or so, the mystique of childhood innocence and the general allure of children have grown considerably. The plight of children often has progressed proportionally with the plight of women, at least until the twentieth century. During this century, women have gradually gained more power and autonomy and have become more actively involved in matters concerning their sexuality. Less and less are they identified with children, who are still viewed as innocent and relatively weak. Because of these qualities, children are seen as being uniquely provocative by many people, particularly those adolescents and adults who are emotionally vulnerable (Nabokov 1955). Children meet these people's need for an innocent and undemanding creature who will not, and indeed cannot, criticize their sexuality and who moreover can be easily overcome through persuasion, manipulation, bribery, or force.

Some of these perpetrators are in highly stressful situations themselves, regressing from more normal and acceptable ways of acting into a pattern that is easier for them to handle. Another group of perpetrators, the pedophiles, have always been fascinated with children and at no time in their lives have successfully engaged in more appropriate intimate relationships with peers. It is not yet known how or why pedophiles develop such tendencies, seemingly at a very early age. What does seem clear, however, is that such people are extremely weak individuals with limited stress-related coping mechanisms and equally limited success in the adult worlds of work and especially relationships. For such people, children are the only people who will give them affection on their own terms.

## The Pursuit of Love and Affection

Frequently, perpetrators cite their own need to be wanted and cared for, which has not been fulfilled in the adult world. In some cases of sexual abuse, particularly in cases of nonviolent contact that has grown over the years from a more normal exchange of tenderness and affection to boundary-breaking sexual behaviors, the overall atmosphere is generally positive, loving, and nurturant, particularly in the beginning stages. Indeed, in a few cases where the child remains ignorant of the magnitude of the problem, the sexual relationship between the child and perpetrator could be masked as a form of love.

Some proponents of incest and sexual relations with children argue that, aside from the "artificial" morals and laws of society, such relationships are as acceptable and as beneficial as other types of intimate or sexual relationships. They declare that the severe social stigma and consequent legal ramifications, along with the "antiquated" morals associated with sex, constitute the real problem. This is an extreme view that ignores the psychological and social factors associated with abuse and its aftermath, but it does contain a grain of truth. Specifically, it suggests that in some cases of sexual abuse, there is a real sense of intimacy and caring, at least for a period of time. For the victim, love, affection, attention, and nurturance may indeed be quite powerful motives for engaging in behavior recognized as being strange or even wrong. This sense of warmth and love is often a major motive for both parties, however perversely it is manifested.

Our society is founded on a fundamental moral assumption that the end does not justify the means. As such, participation in sexually exploitive behaviors, despite the importance or value of love, warmth, and affection, is fundamentally wrong and immoral (Forward 1978; Geiser 1979). Children in this society are considered unable to make rational and informed choices concerning sexual behavior, particularly when they are in their preteen years. Forceful or manipulative participation in such activities is therefore deemed both wrong and illegal and is subject to moral and legal sanction. Obviously, there are some gray areas in respect to this matter. For example, a fairly independent and mature seventeen-year-old who becomes involved in an affair with her stepuncle might be entering the relationship with a high degree of awareness and control and for reasons no different from most of her peers or other young adults. This girl is legally a minor, however, and the case is potentially subject to the same rules as one involving a seven-year-old girl. Obviously, the two situations are markedly different, but the legal system could deal with them in the same way.

## Power and Control

These motives are most frequently observed in association with anger and rape. Almost all cases of sexual abuse contain some degree of power in the sense that the perpetrator typically asserts his or her authority in the overall process of manipulation and seduction. At times this power surfaces in direct ways, with the perpetrator imposing or suggesting the use of force, either during the sexual abuse itself or as a threat against revealing what has happened. Occasionally, a perpetrator will act in a distinctly violent manner that we call rape. Rape, defined as an act of sexual violence, occurs in many sexual abuse cases, although to varying degrees. The use of overt violence in child sexual abuse is generally uncommon, however, mainly because children are often ignorant of what they are doing and act obediently out of a learned submission to authority.

It can be argued that the perpetrator exercises his or her power and control in one form or another in every occurrence of sexual abuse, particularly if manipulation and seduction are considered expressions of power. Perpetrators typically need some sense of power in their lives, especially power resulting in others' compliance with their whims, to counteract their overriding sense of powerlessness. Failing to accomplish this in the world of their peers, perpetrators turn to children to satisfy this need.

## Conclusion

Although these factors do not fully explain why individuals sexually abuse children, they do provide a framework for the most common dynamics involved in such cases. In fact, we might know more about the dynamics of sexual abuse than about the equally pervasive crimes of aggression, violence, and theft. The problem of evil has haunted humanity over the ages. All religions and philosophies have addressed this problem, with little common agreement. Scientists have examined the brains of criminals, psychoanalysts and other therapists have explored criminals' minds and unconscious desires, and countless investigators have detailed the complicated family and life experiences that have led perpetrators to commit antisocial acts. Despite these explorations, there are no simple reasons for any major violation of the prevailing mode of conduct within a culture. Sexual abuse is no exception.

# 13

# Prevention of Sexual Abuse

THIS book is primarily concerned with the treatment of sexual abuse cases after they have occurred, but it is important to address the general issue of prevention for two reasons: first, to prevent future episodes of abuse involving the parties involved in a particular episode; second, to prevent abuse of or by other children and, by extension, future adults. The guidelines and strategies suggested here are extremely important to implement in families, schools, churches, health care practices, and other organizations dealing directly with children. Remember that *children can frequently prevent or stop sexual abuse in many cases.*

This chapter does not purport to review all aspects of prevention programs, but rather presents the main principles of most programs (see also Adams and Fay 1981; Sanford 1980). Appendix A provides references to more complete programs, which contain specific exercises pertinent to particular age groups. The following suggestions are broken down into eight categories: privacy, personal rights, sexuality and sexual expression, social interactions, supervision, child care, communication, and postabuse prevention. See appendix B for relevant readings for children, appendix C for relevant readings for parents and trainers, and appendix D for audiovisual productions.

## Privacy

Talk to children at various times about the distinction between what is private and what is public, particularly with respect to bodily functioning.

Help children express their need for privacy when desired or needed, and teach them acceptable mechanisms for fulfilling this need.

Make sure children have access to private places in the house and school. Allow for closed, and possibly locked, doors; if concrete barriers are not present, help children find some way of gaining increased privacy.

Respect the privacy of the bathroom, ensuring each person in the family or classroom strict privacy when he or she is engaged in private activities therein (unless someone clearly needs or asks for assistance).

Be careful about sexually ambiguous household matters between adults and children, using as guides appropriate societal and religious standards whenever possible. Activities such as parents or relatives appearing nude in front of children or taking baths or showers with them should be increasingly restricted as children advance in age. Furthermore, it is generally a good idea for the same sex parent to bathe a child after the age of four, especially in the case of adult males and female children. From the age of three or so, the child should be expected to wash his or her own private parts.

## Personal Rights

Talk to children about the different types of touches. Good touches include mutually desirable physical contact, such as hugging, tickling, signs of affection, or physical contact in sports and other games. Bad touches include unwanted touches that either hurt, feel funny, invade regions of privacy, or cause confusion. Let children know that it is their right not to be subjected to bad touches. If they are confused about the meaning of a particular touch, children should be told to ask someone they trust about it.

Encourage children to make active decisions about when and by whom they want to be touched. Dissuade them from being objects for someone else's (especially an adult's) gratification.

Teach children to respect the rights of other people in general, regardless of age, sex, race, culture, physical or mental condition, or personality. Similarly, teach them about their individual right to be free from exploitation and abuse.

Talk to children about friendships they have with other people. Encourage them to talk to you or another caring authority figure about anything that is bothersome or confusing in those relationships.

Encourage children to report any abuse of or by friends or acquaintances.

Tell children they are not to blame if they are touched or otherwise abused by others. Tell them that it is the other person's fault.

A polite child is not always a safe child. Give children permission to say no and to defy or question authority if the authority figure is doing something that makes them uncomfortable.

## Sexuality and Sexual Expression

Talk to children about sexuality, providing them with sex education that is suitable to their age and mental abilities. Do not make sexuality and sexual parts of the body a taboo subject. Help children talk comfortably about their whole body.

Convince preadolescent children not to share in keeping secrets with adults or older children and adolescents in regard to sexual matters. Talk to adolescents about when they should inform and when privacy should be respected. Tell all children and adolescents to be especially suspicious whenever anyone touches them and cautions them not to tell.

Give children clear rules and standards about sexual behavior, encouraging them to talk openly with someone they trust about topics of interest or concern. It is important to allow normal sexual curiosity and sexual play to occur while at the same time preventing abusive encounters. Start with fairly clear and rigid standards at an early age, followed by a gradual transition to increased independence and decision making in sexual matters as children mature and gain responsibility.

Restrict children's access to films, television shows, books, pictures, or magazines that openly display sexual behavior. If you are in doubt, view the show or read the book along with the children, discussing related feelings, opinions, and experiences.

Be aware of various physical interactions that could eroticize children's feelings and result in abnormal sexual arousal. Restrict or avoid exposure to such situations. These include activities such as spanking (especially on the bare bottom), bodily embarrassment (being spanked as above with others watching), enemas, observation of direct sex (expecially sex between parents, the so-called primal scene), sensual massage (especially involving breasts, buttocks, or genitals), prolonged or passionate kissing, and requested modeling or adoption of provocative postures.

While always encouraging open communication in terms of sexuality, give children clear rules in respect to sexual behavior, warning of strict consequences if they willfully misbehave. This naturally has to be adapted to the particular child, family, and culture, as children too fearful of consequences might be unwilling to talk about abuse. In general, however, it is important to let children know that sexual behavior that violates the rules is not acceptable.

Watch for any signs of drastic changes in sexual behavior, including new behaviors and significant changes in old behaviors. Excessive masturbation is often an indication of abuse, especially if it is conducted publicly, compulsively, or flagrantly.

Expose children to suitable books, programs, or trained adults who can be helpful in answering more detailed questions or providing added information in regard to sex education and abuse. Provide them with the names of other people to whom they can turn with questions, problems, or concerns.

When talking to children about sexuality, use appropriate books, drawings, and diagrams. Also use the proper terminology whenever possible, conveying the sense that sexuality is a normal function of one's body. It is important to demystify sexuality so that it becomes a topic more open for discussion.

In all discussions of sexuality and sexual behavior, be sure to stress the fact that sex is a normal part of the human condition and that sex itself is not bad but that certain sexual practices are wrong and harmful. These practices include forced sex of any kind, as well as manipulation, deceit, trickery, exploitation, taking advantage of a younger or more innocent person, betrayal of trust, and aggressive attacks.

Accept children's normal sexual behavior (see chapter 2), or at least discuss it calmly, citing appropriate moral concerns. Abnormal sexual behavior should be treated as symptomatic of some problem, such as sexual abuse, and not punished but instead discussed in detail.

Do not force affection on children or force them to be affectionate with others.

## Social Interactions

Give children clear and concrete steps to take if someone tries to touch or abuse them or tells them to do things they think are wrong or make them feel uncomfortable. Practice specific verbal and physical responses to various hypothetical situations of this nature.

Help children deal with manipulation and seduction in its many guises, particularly when bribery, secrecy, uncomfortable feelings, or bad touches occur.

Help children deal with relationships stemming from family changes, especially relationships with half siblings or steprelatives.

Advise children not to play or take rides with strangers. If a stranger asks the child to do something, instruct the child to say no or to ask an adult in charge first. Try not to inspire undue fear of strangers; rather, focus on having children check with someone else if at all in doubt about what to do.

Help children say no in different ways, giving them particular reasons for doing so and explaining the consequences.

Let children know that even people they know, trust, respect, and love, including parents, relatives, teachers, friends, baby-sitters, and other authority figures, might be guilty of bad touches. Tell them that if this occurs, they should contact someone else. Naturally, care should be taken to assure children that most of the people they respect are indeed trustworthy.

Play "what if" games with children. Pose various social problems and listen to their responses, guiding and coaching them when necessary.

Tell children that it is okay to scream for help or run away from danger if confronted by someone who makes them feel uncomfortable. Tell them to run to a place where there are a lot of people.

Do not dress children in ways that make them stand out from peers, particularly in expensive or high-fashion clothing.

Do not put personalized names on children's clothing, lunch boxes, or backpacks in conspicuous ways.

## Supervision

Convince children that they should tell you or another responsible adult if they are experiencing bad touches or if someone is asking them to touch them in bad or uncomfortable ways.

Be aware of what children in your charge are doing and where they are at all times. If they are not under your direct supervision, make sure someone you trust is in charge.

Be alert to any stranger who seems to be spending an excessive amount of time alone with your children, children in your charge, or children in general. Closer scrutiny and investigation of such a situation, and discussion with the children involved, is in order.

Tell children where you will be at all times and where you or your substitute can be reached. Also, give children access to other people whom they can contact in times of distress.

Alert children to the fact that sexual abuse is wrong and illegal, making sure they understand the concept and its manifestations and know precisely what to do if abuse occurs or is suspected.

Assure children that they can turn to you in times of need or distress. Be available when they need you, making definite suggestions and giving clear advice at such times.

Evaluate children's walking routes and play areas for places of potential hazard, danger, or entrapment.

Check out any suspicious people or enterprises in the community.

Maintain a clear and consistent approach to discipline and standards, helping children operate within a well-defined moral context that allows them to distinguish clearly between right and wrong.

No children under six years of age should ever be left unsupervised. Older children should be supervised most of the time and always have someone nearby to whom they can turn if they need help.

Young children should not play alone outdoors for any length of time.

Teach children to look for someone in charge when they are lost, preferably someone who is wearing a uniform or has clear authority.

Be aware of any apparent emotional or behavioral changes in children, as well as any unusual or valuable gifts they might have received. At such times, it is very important to discuss what is happening with the child, providing a structure and model for open and honest communication.

## Child Care

Check on references for all caretakers and baby-sitters. Observe them, directly and indirectly, interacting with your child. Talk to your child afterward about his or her experiences with the care-taker.

Carefully examine the procedures, curriculum, and personnel of any organized child-care provider or program. Make sure any such provider is licensed, reputable, and competent. Talk to other parents about their experiences, asking them to list positive and nega-tive points.

Do not give blanket permission for trips, outings, activities, and discipline. Make sure you are satisfied with procedures, guidelines, restraint, and informed consent.

Make sure that you can drop in unannounced at any time, within some general guidelines, to observe, visit, or participate. Indeed, do so on occasion.

Make sure your child will be released only to you or others whom you specifically mention. Notify the school of any changes in schedule, particularly in regard to pickup at the end of the day.

Keep a list, preferably in common with trustworthy friends or neighbors, of reliable and competent baby-sitters. Occasionally, share information, opinions, and suggestions with other parents.

Clarify bedtime procedures with baby-sitters, stressing the impor-tance of keeping to general guidelines.

Clarify the responsibilities of the baby-sitter, as well as permissible activities. Pay particular attention to his or her other social interac-tions, such as phone calls and visits from friends.

Alert all caretakers to your precise whereabouts, other people whom they can contact in time of need, and telephone numbers where you can be reached.

Be comfortable with the care your child will receive if he or she stays overnight someplace. Make sure one or more adults whom you trust is in charge of the house during that time.

For older children and adolescents who go out by themselves at night, be sure you know the nature of their activities, where they can be reached, and any supervisory arrangements, especially if they will be visiting other people's houses. Limits as to behavior, curfew, activities, and friends should be discussed and agreed on beforehand, with related consequences for disobedience clearly spelled out.

## Communication

Honest communication should be highly valued. An open confession of a bad action, whether in regard to abuse or any other matter, should be met with less severe consequences than a willfully kept secret.

Stress the difference between secrets and surprises (the latter can eventually be revealed), minimizing the need for secrets. Moreover, tell children that bad secrets (secrets that make them uncomfortable) should be shared.

Convey to children a sense of trust and honesty by being direct and honest with them and indicating that you hope they will be the same way with you. Related to this, always believe children are telling the truth unless you have specific information to the contrary, particularly about matters of sexuality and sexual abuse. In general, stress that you will believe them.

Encourage children to be assertive in expressing feelings and opinions, both with you and with other people.

Make sure children know their names, addresses, home phone number, the emergency number (911), the operator number (0), and your work number. Review this information with them periodically and have them practice using the phone.

Give children a secret code word by which they can recognize whether another person has legitimate approval of parents or caretakers. Since this code word would only be known to the parents and child, anyone who uses it presumably has the approval of parents.

Listen to any strange statements made by children. In particular, be alert to things children might *not* be saying or disclosing.

Encourage children to find adults and children with whom they can discuss highly personal feelings and confusing or negative experiences.

Talk to children frequently about topics that are emotionally arousing or meaningful to them. These might include television programs, stories, nightmares, real-life crises, or news broadcasts.

## Postabuse Prevention

If a child has been a victim, help him or her understand the importance of talking to you or a counselor about feelings concerning sexual behavior and relevant interpersonal relationships. Victims of sexual abuse frequently have problems with sexual behavior, requiring constant and helpful dialogue with supportive and caring persons.

If a child has been an offender, help him or her realize that you will be available to talk and in general be more aware of the child's activities. Be firm in following through on clearly defined consequences if such behavior continues.

If a spouse has been guilty of abuse with one or more of your children, immediately seek help not only for your spouse, but also for your marriage. Whether you are aware of it or not, there is most likely a major problem in your relationship.

If a colleague has molested a child, try not to spread gossip or otherwise denigrate the person. Rather, consider the offender to be someone who has a serious emotional problem for which he or she needs help and support. Let the person's actions and discussions with you, not what you know of his or her other problems, determine your relationship.

If a relative has molested one or more of your children, encourage him or her to get help. Also try to decrease the inevitable family tension that will ensue, particularly if the relative denies doing anything harmful.

If a friend has been guilty of abuse, be supportive and caring, meanwhile strongly encouraging him or her to get help. Try not to think badly of the person, but certainly do not condone his or her actions.

If abuse has occurred in your immediate nuclear family, attempt to deal with it openly and honestly, accepting it as a mistake and wrong but developing communication and boundaries that will prevent future episodes.

Help the child and family deal with the possible social aftermath of abuse, both in terms of decreasing its painful effects and coping with any negative stigma or reputation associated with the abuse.

# 14

# Counseling

A COMMON concern of parents and teachers is whether to seek outside help for a child's emotional state in the wake of sexual abuse. They are frequently concerned about both short-term and long-term effects and often feel the child might find it easier to talk with a caring professional outside the immediate family and school who has experience dealing with such cases. To some people, however, counseling (used synonymously with *therapy* in this chapter) is a sign of weakness or sickness. They do not believe that it is necessary or helpful.

## General Guidelines

Although there are no definite guidelines of when to seek professional help, counseling can be quite useful in a variety of circumstances:

Counseling can be used as a diagnostic aid to determine more precisely the circumstances, details, events, and interactional behaviors that precipitated, occurred during, and stemmed from the sexual abuse.

Counseling might help the child to vent his or her feelings in direct, open, spontaneous, and expressive ways without fear of retribution or negative repercussions.

Experienced counselors use many different techniques to help children express feelings. Typically, they use paths of least resistance, thereby making it easy for the child to disclose his or her feelings and work through problems.

Counseling can explore feelings in more intimate and confidential ways than similar discussions with friends, relatives, or nuclear family members. The counselor is often trained to be extremely sensitive to a child's emotional state, and the child can freely express himself or herself because he or she probably will not be affected either directly or indirectly in future encounters.

Counselors trained in sexual abuse cases have a variety of resources, such as books, films, and activities, available to them.

Counselors who specialize in sexual abuse cases have heard it all, thereby allowing the child to be completely open without worrying about the emotional effects his or her statements will have on the counselor.

The counselor can give the child specific advice about how to handle future interactions, emotional distress, relationships with peers and family, and any other areas of concern.

Counseling can help the child better identify support structures and perhaps even help mobilize these structures in the child's behalf.

Counseling helps children realize that they are not alone, as counselors often provide materials detailing other children's experiences and sometimes ask children to participate in group sessions with others who have had similar experiences.

Counselors often have considerable power in dealing with the larger systems involved in the child's life, including the family, social and legal services, and the school.

Counseling can be of considerable assistance in helping families deal with marital and family dynamics, especially in incest cases, and in encouraging family support, coping, and management systems.

Counseling can help all people be better prepared for future situations of a similar nature, giving training and advice in the area of prevention.

Counseling can be of great assistance in helping offenders recognize the dynamics of the abuse and develop alternative strategies for dealing with the emotional arousal they associate with the abusive encounter.

Forensic evaluations, as a particular type of mental health assessment, can be of great service in addressing specific details of the sexual abuse to be used in court, often in lieu of the more grueling direct testimony of the child. This is distinguished from the first use of counseling in that this kind of evaluation is specifically meant to be documented in a written form and disseminated to the proper authorities to help them make legal and treatment decisions regarding the case. Unlike the former, this is not highly confidential.

Counseling can help all parties involved in a case express their feelings, work through emotional blocks, employ helpful coping skills, reduce tension, learn alternative and more productive ways of acting in the future, become more assertive in language and action, and minimize long-term negative effects and the risk of similar experiences recurring.

In general, it is advisable for all children and adolescents who are either victims or offenders to see a professional counselor at least once (James and Nasjleti 1983; Walters 1975). Although some cases are handled quite well by the child, family, and relevant community support people and do not require the assistance of outside helping professionals, this ideal situation rarely exists. Unfortunately, the natural systems within which the child is involved often play a significant part in the problem. These are hardly neutral contexts, being greatly affected by the situation and in turn affecting the child's ability to be completely open or feel completely supported. Counseling is thus a way to obtain sufficient support from a relatively neutral yet positive source.

## Special Situations

While some form of counseling is recommended for all cases, it is *essential* in the following:

Children who have been repeatedly abused over a long period of time by one or more offenders

Children who have suffered a particularly traumatic form of abuse, especially those cases in which there was a significant amount of aggression, humiliation, or embarrassment

Children and adolescents who have been previously abused and have subsequently become offenders

All cases of incest within the nuclear family

All cases in which there are significant short-term effects and intense symptoms such as nightmares, bed-wetting, flashbacks, phobias, or anxiety attacks

All cases in which the child wants to talk with an outside professional

Cases in which family members need advice and support in dealing with the situation

Cases in which there will be forthcoming legal action of a contested nature in which the child might be called on to testify

## Techniques and Duration

Counselors use a variety of techniques in working with children and adolescents who have been involved in sexual abuse (National Center on Child Abuse and Neglect 1980). They employ some of the techniques described in previous chapters but typically have access to a wider range of materials and methods. Most often, the path of least resistance to expression is chosen by the counselor as the medium of communication. For younger children, more nonverbal techniques are commonly used, whereas for older children and adolescents, verbal methods are most commonly used. In all cases, occasional use of art, verbal discussion, play, role playing, and empathic listening to information or materials presented are components of the therapeutic process. Depending on the age and intelligence of the child, the counselor will help the child gain insight into the often complex interpersonal dynamics involved, as well as the child's own complex and ambivalent feelings. Various strategies of action and expression are used in the sessions and encouraged outside sessions to enable the child to vent her or his feelings and achieve a more balanced view of the matter.

Duration of counseling depends on the nature of the case, with more complex cases taking substantially more time than simple or circumscribed cases. To the extent that incestuous family dynamics are involved, for example, many more issues must be resolved than in the case of an isolated abusive encounter with a neighbor or babysitter. The intensity and trauma of the event itself, as well as the amount of time that passed between the abuse incident and reporting, also affect the nature and duration of counseling.

Most often, counselors work directly with the child victim or offender, but at times they try to involve the family and other support systems. Some counselors prefer working directly and mainly with the family, particularly in matters of incest. Other counselors advocate group counseling for children, which exposes them to others who have had similar experiences. Although counseling techniques and styles differ, all counselors are primarily trying to help the child express his or her feelings in honest and thorough ways, to help the child learn more appropriate and effective coping and protection mechanisms, to mobilize support structures, to provide immediate relief of symptoms, and to help various people gain better insight and understanding into the particular and general dynamics involved.

## Finding a Counselor

Counseling services are available in most communities, but it is important to select a counselor who has had suitable experience and sufficient training in matters of child sexual abuse. For the most part, counselors and therapists who specialize in child or adolescent therapy and who are licensed or certified in their respective disciplines are typically able to handle most sexual abuse cases. For more specialized endeavors, such as forensic evaluations or treatment of a very specific symptom, more critical selection techniques should be used. At times, school guidance counselors and psychologists can be quite helpful in addressing some of the issues. Occasionally, they even conduct group and individual counseling within the school context. For the most part, however, sexual abuse cases are best treated in outpatient mental health clinics that employ personnel trained in child and adolescent therapy in general and sexual abuse cases in particular.

Most insurance plans that include coverage of mental health problems will pay for visits to such counselors, many of whom have sliding fee schedules if financial situations so indicate. Moreover, many state service programs offer their own financial and therapeutic assistance in such cases and can usually provide you with names of skilled counselors.

# 15

# Frequently Asked Questions

AT times, parents and teachers ask specific questions concerning a sexual abuse incident. Some of these questions appear in this chapter, along with answers that you might find beneficial.

## Parents

*Will my child ever forget what happened?*

No one ever forgets a trauma, but with the proper care, support system, and self-esteem builders, your child will learn coping techniques that will lessen the trauma and make life less fearful, negative, and depressing.

*Will my child ever be normal?*

Your child is normal; it was the ordeal your child experienced that was abnormal, causing subsequent problems in your child's emotions and actions. As with any trauma, having someone to talk with who has either been in the same situation or is experienced in talking with victims is often comforting and can be helpful in the healing process.

*My child said to me while we were playing, "Daddy, that's a bad touch." I froze. What should I have said or done?*

First, ask your child what touch caused a bad feeling. Second, discuss the situation. Third, thank your child for trusting you and telling you that a certain touch felt wrong. This process will allow your child to confide and communicate openly with you.

*How long will my child need to be in treatment?*

Since the circumstances of each offense and the personality and related coping styles of each child are different, only the therapist working with your child can determine the severity of the trauma, expected course of therapy, and general prognosis.

*My child is currently having problems getting along with people he used to get along with. Is this related to his being sexually abused?*

A sexually abused child goes through many different stages after the trauma. Your child might not trust people he once did. He might feel that everyone knows what happened, and therefore he wants to withdraw. Other variables also might be determining his behavior, however, such as the onset of puberty. Talk with your child, tell him you have noticed that he is unable to get along with others, and observe his response. If he continues to be uncooperative and antagonistic, seek professional help.

*Will my child tend to be a victim in the future now that this has happened?*

Victim behavior is often learned after a trauma because of the helplessness your child felt during the ordeal and the modeling he or she experienced. Whether this type of behavior will continue in the future depends on what type of offense occurred, how long it occurred, and with whom it occurred. You might want to enroll your child in an assertiveness class or sport such as karate or basketball to help him or her overcome some of his or her fear or perceived lack of control.

*Should I talk about what happened? If so, when?*

If your child starts to talk about what happened, stop, listen, and answer his or her questions as they are asked. If you bring up the topic, your child might not want to discuss it, tending to get angry or irritated. If you are concerned that abuse is recurring, then certainly bring up the topic. Let your child know you are interested in her or his well-being, even if the child does not want to hear it or pretends not to be listening. Always be tactful and sensitive.

*Why didn't my child tell me?*

The perpetrator might have threatened your child's life or your life. Perhaps your child was afraid of punishment or blame if he or she told. Your child might want to protect you or might feel guilt or loyalty, not wanting to tattle or squeal. Whatever the reason, your child was acting out of fear, and that fear was stronger than anything else.

*What is normal "doctor play" in young children, and what is abnormal?*

Most young children play doctor. This usually includes showing and touching each other's genitals because of curiosity. Remembering that sexual abuse is an abuse of power is helpful in determining whether your child's doctor play is normal. If any child uses his or her power to intimidate or make another child do something that scares, hurts, or otherwise causes distress, it is abnormal and should be investigated.

*I've heard that almost all offenders were previous victims of abuse. How can I prevent my child from becoming an offender?*

It is essential that your child get treatment. Make sure the professional who provides the treatment has worked with victims of sexual abuse and is knowledgeable about the dynamics involved. The earlier treatment occurs, the better the outcome will be, as the victim will have less time to deny what happened and begin to work through the trauma as soon as possible. Offenders who were previously abused have never worked through their problems.

*My son has a habit of making up stories. How do I know he is not doing the same thing about being fondled?*

Most children do not falsify facts regarding sexual molestation. The only time we have seen children lie about being sexually abused is in custody cases, and that only occasionally. Here are some factors to consider when deciding whether or not your child is telling the truth:

Is your child's story consistent over repeated tellings?

Have you noticed any symptoms or behavioral changes in your child?

Is your child's story detailed in such a realistic way, especially concerning sexual activity?

Have you or anyone else observed any deviant sexual acting out in your child that is concurrent with your child's telling you what happened?

In general, it is important always to believe your child regarding sexually abusive situations unless there is clear evidence to show that your child is fabricating the story.

*A member of our extended family abused our child. How should we handle contact with relatives?*

If the perpetrator admits his or her guilt, takes full responsibility for the offense, and gets help, contact with the relatives, including the perpetrator, is acceptable as long as your child is supervised and does not display any behavioral symptoms or express fears regarding the situation. This contact should be limited to special events such as holidays, birthdays, weddings, and funerals. Everyday activities should be severely restricted, at least for a while. If the perpetrator does not admit his or her guilt, no contact should be allowed.

*Should I check up on the treatment of the offender, especially if I know him or her?*

You definitely should obtain information regarding the offense, whether the perpetrator is denying the offense, and the prognosis for recovery. During the treatment process, the perpetrator should make a verbal, sincere apology to the victim. The confidentiality of offenders who are in treatment should *not* be kept because it enhances their denial system.

*My eight-year-old child seems extremely interested in sex and bathroom matters and gets excited or giggly when such topics are brought up. Is this a sign that she's been abused?*

Most eight-year-olds are interested in sex and find toilet jokes very funny. Most are extremely giggly and embarrassed when such topics are brought up. Only if your child exhibits unusual behavior regarding sex should you suspect that she has been abused.

*Should I tell my child that I was sexually abused when I was a child?*

Yes, you should tell your child, especially when teaching your child personal safety, but your child should be old enough not to feel afraid about what you are telling him or her. You should *not* give details or be overly emotional. If your intention is to instill fear or elicit a specific response, then your motive is misguided. Sharing this experience will help you and your child prevent abuse from happening again. Your child will probably appreciate your openness and feel closer to you.

*Will my child have to take the stand in court and be subject to harsh cross-examination?*

Your child might have to take the stand and be cross-examined, but changes such as videotaping your child's testimony and appointing neutral investigators whose reports are acceptable as evidence in court might be possible in lieu of direct testimony. The introduction of family court systems will no doubt help alleviate this continuing victimization of the child.

*A neighborhood child told me that she is being sexually abused. What should I do?*

The child was crying out for help. Tell the child that you must report this information to the state agency mandated to deal with the sexual

abuse of children. It is essential that an investigation into this allegation be made to determine its validity and get help for the child.

*My boyfriend has admitted that he's been sexually abusing my daughter.
He wants to get help for all of us and seems genuinely sorry. I believe he
wants to change and I am willing to enter counseling with him, but neither
of us wants this reported to outside authorities. Can it be kept a secret between
ourselves and our counselor?*

The law in most states mandates that any counselor, therapist, medical doctor, nurse, teacher, minister, or mental health professional must
report any sexual abuse case (or even reasonable suspicion thereof) or
be subject to arrest and prosecution. Therefore, this offense cannot
be kept a secret and must be reported. In the long run, this is a much
safer course for you, your child, and society. Most offenders are simply *not* motivated enough to change their behavior without a high
degree of external pressure. Also, the abuse might happen again and
might have occurred with other children besides your own.

*My wife and I are divorced. She has become a lesbian, and my son is
exposed to her women friends. Will this affect him?*

Your son might be affected by exposure to your ex-wife's women
friends if he witnessed or was subjected to their sexual activity, if he
were teased by his peers, or if he felt caught in the middle of a divorce
battle. Otherwise, your son probably will not be harmed by your ex-
wife's lifestyle, as long as you are not unduly critical of her, especially
in front of your son.

*Our daughter has been receiving obscene phone calls after school before we
come home from work, and they have been terrifying to her. What should
we do?*

The most important thing is your daughter's safety; therefore, the
ideal situation is not to allow your daughter to be home alone. Either
find an after-school program or get a baby-sitter to come into your
home. Obtaining an unlisted telephone number and reporting the in-

cidents to the police are essential in relieving your daughter's fears and possibly identifying the obscene caller.

*I recently found a bunch of nude magazines in my son's room. What should I do?*

Your moral standards and rules, along with the type of nude magazines, will determine how you should handle this situation. If your child is a preteen, you should ask why he is hiding the magazines, where he got them, and how you feel about his viewing them. Young children usually do not understand nude magazines and should not be exposed to them. You might feel differently if your child is a teenager, but you should question your child about them and decide whether you want such magazines in the house. Open discussion is helpful in either case, as there might be more appropriate and less exploitive ways of satisfying your son's sexual curiosity.

*I just found out my son sexually abused a neighborhood girl. What should I do?*

Your first reaction might be to physically punish him for what he did, but you should realize that your son might also be a victim of sexual abuse. Instead of punishing him, ask him, "Who sexually abused you, and when did it happen?" Do not ask your son, "Have you ever been sexually abused?" Most likely, he will deny that any deviant sexual behavior occurred because of the suggestion that he might be gay. Your son no doubt interprets this sexual violation as a loss of power and masculinity; therefore, an admission that such an experience occurred will be difficult. Be firm in your questioning.

Whether or not you find out that your son has been victimized, immediately report the incident(s) to the proper authorities, then find your son the proper treatment program. He must learn to be responsible for his actions and needs treatment to resolve his own possible victimization. Your reaction is vital in providing him with the security and strength to admit his victimization, realize that he needs treatment to alleviate his pain, and stop him from becoming a chronic offender.

*How should I advise my child to deal with strangers?*

Although certain rules should be established, such as not going for a ride with a stranger without explicit parental consent, parents should not inspire too much fear of strangers, as many people mean well and are genuinely interested in children. Children should be told that if anything appears suspicious, particularly if they are told to keep questionable secrets or if they experience uncomfortable feelings, they should avoid contact with the specific stranger(s) and inform parents or other trusted adults.

## Teachers

Teachers come into frequent contact with children who are physically, sexually, or emotionally abused. These children come from families of all economic levels and social strata, but all such families have significant problems and stress, sometimes in crisis proportions. If teachers are alert to the signs and symptoms of abuse, they can take the first steps in helping the children. A teacher must be prepared to deal with both the educational and the emotional side of the student. The following are questions frequently asked by teachers regarding victimized children.

*I have a fifth-grade student who had been sexually abused by many different perpetrators. My class is arranged in cooperative learning groups. This child prefers to sit in the corner away from everyone. Should I allow her to do this?*

Everyone needs some time by himself or herself, but this child appears not to trust anyone and fears intimacy. She probably feels more secure by herself because she knows what to expect. She must have a positive learning experience, however, as well as positive interpersonal relationships. Set specific rules with her and the entire class regarding accepting group time and individual time. Strongly reinforce this child's every attempt to work with the group. She probably needs a great deal of positive reinforcement and nurturance to be successful. Be firm with rules and gentle in manner.

*One of my first-grade students came to me and said, "My baby-sitter makes me touch his penis." He does not want to go home. What should I do?*

First, you must believe the child. Do not send him home to the baby-sitter. Take the boy to the principal's office and ask him to tell the principal what he told you. It is the principal's responsibility to call the appropriate authorities and report this case. It is your responsibility to report to the school principal, nurse, or guidance counselor.

*Tommy is an extremely angry child. He pushes everyone around. Yesterday he confessed that he had been abused by his mother's boyfriend. Do I treat him differently from the other children?*

The same classroom rules and consequences for breaking the rules that apply to the other children in your class also apply to Tommy. The difference is that Tommy will need more reminders of the rules and associated consequences, along with a more consistent follow-through. Tommy also will need many more positive reinforcers because statistics have shown that for every negative experience one encounters, it takes many more positive experiences to regain the same level of self-confidence.

*Jennifer is ten years old. She is constantly picking at her skin until it bleeds. Her social worker reported that Jennifer has been sexually and physically abused. What can I do to help her at school?*

Observe Jennifer for a few days. Note the times she does not pick her skin and also the times she picks her skin the most. Implement a behavior modification program that will positively reinforce Jennifer for not picking her skin. Most children like praise, stickers, or a certificate of achievement. You will be the best judge of what will work with Jennifer. Another suggestion is to involve Jennifer in a group that addresses self-esteem. See if your guidance counselor or local mental health professional can help.

*I have a child in my class who has been sexually abused and has been diagnosed as emotionally disturbed. I do not have any background in deal-*

*ing with this mental health condition. I am nervous that I might say or do something that will make her lose control. What do I do?*

Meet with any professionals who have dealt with this child. Review the information and evaluations and ask for recommendations to assist you in providing the best educational program and learning environment for the child. If a problem arises that you cannot handle, enlist help from the principal, guidance counselor, or anyone else who is available.

*Tara is a six-year-old who came to our school in the middle of the year. She had been placed in foster care after her father allegedly sexually molested her. She is fearful of everything and cries easily. I want to gain her trust. How can I do this?*

Be consistent and structured when working with Tara. Never make any promises to her that you cannot fulfill. Most likely, she will test you to see whether you will fail her. It is imperative that you are honest with her. Gaining Tara's trust will be a long process, and it might never occur. However, every positive interpersonal relationship will help increase Tara's trust, at least to some extent.

*Billy constantly complains of stomachaches. The school nurse insists that nothing is physically wrong with him. Last year Billy's mother served a jail sentence for sexually abusing him. She is not allowed to have any contact with him. How can I make school enjoyable for him?*

Billy might need the services of a psychologist regarding his victimization, somatic complaints, and lack of contact with his mother. If he is not receiving outside services, refer him to the guidance counselor. Whether Billy will be successful in your class depends on many factors. The most important thing you can do is to focus on the positive and reinforce Billy's every attempt to participate.

*I have three students who have been identified as having been sexually abused. All three have emotional and learning problems. Am I supposed to be an educator, a therapist, or both?*

As an educator, you are one of the most significant people in your students' lives. Because so many children have experienced abuse, you will be encountering more students in your classroom who have been abused. Therefore, you need to know the dynamics of abuse and the short- and long-term effects on the child.

# Appendix A:
# Strategies for Reducing Stress in Children

*Donald Hillman*
*Sally Blakeslee Ives*

1. Be aware that certain changes are quite normal, and usually temporary, reactions to stress. These changes include the following:
   a. Increased anxiety
   b. Confusion and uncertainty
   c. Use of coping and defense mechanisms
   d. Aggravation of preexisting problems
   e. Decreased efficiency and task performance
   f. Diverse physical or stress-related (psychosomatic) symptoms
   g. Regression to earlier patterns of behavior

   If any of these changes becomes too great, causing the child to be out of control, then either intervention or consultation should be considered.

2. It is important to talk to the child about the stressful situation, allowing the child to express his or her ideas, opinions, feelings, worries, and concerns.

3. It is far less helpful to give the child your own ideas, feelings, and opinions than it is to help the child sort out his or her own. It is beneficial, however, to introduce the child to new perspectives on the situation. Try less to give simple, black-and-white answers than to help the child see different sides and draw his or her own conclusions.

4. Be alert to the child's particular way(s) of coping with stress and assist him or her in employing these mechanisms in the most useful and constructive manner.

5. Expect that grades, marks, and scores might slip a little, due to the stress itself as well as to the changes occurring following the abuse.

6. Allow increased time for family and group activities in general, as social support is helpful in times of stress.

7. Spend more time with the child in mutually enjoyable activities. Refrain from talking about the stress unless the child brings it up or you feel the time is suitable.

8. Encourage activities allowing for physical exercise and release of tension. Both competitive and cooperative games, albeit for different reasons, are equally helpful.

9. In general, it is most useful to focus on, talk about, and deal directly with the stress when the child is either acutely upset or very relaxed. Stress reduction seems to be most helpful, incidentally, when the stress is dealt with at both times.

10. Assist the child in gaining understanding and control whenever reasonable, at least to the extent possible given the conditions. Be particularly assertive in not allowing the child to feel hopelessly out of control or otherwise victimized. There are many ways of capturing some control cognitively, emotionally, and behaviorally.

11. Help the child brainstorm creative courses of action for himself or herself, for other children, and maybe even for adults.

12. Encourage the child to talk with other children about the situation.

13. Encourage the child to read, listen to, or view fictional stories of true accounts of how other children have coped with similar stress.

14. Counsel and advise the child about ways of handling particular sources of stress, such as feeling in the middle, actually observing some of the conflict, being criticized, or feeling pulled in two

directions. It seems best to focus on helping the child stand his or her own ground to avoid being pulled back and forth and caught in the middle.

15. Encourage the child to express his or her thoughts, feelings, and concerns—for example, by writing in a private journal or making things of a creative nature (drawing, sculpting, doodling, building, and so on).

16. To the extent possible, increase the child's security by following a predictable routine and being reliable and consistent within the family.

# Appendix B:
# Materials for Children

*Acquaintance Rape: Awareness and Prevention for Teenagers* by Py Bateman. Available from Alternatives to Fear, Seattle, WA. A workbook for adolescents explaining acquaintance rape and various specific action techniques that teenagers can use to prevent such an event.

*Alice Doesn't Babysit Anymore* by Kevin McGovern. Available from McGovern and Mulbacker Books in Portland, OR. A story about a female baby-sitter who abuses children, containing advice on what to do if someone you trust attempts to molest you.

*Dear Elizabeth* by Gene Mackey and Helen Swan. Available from the Children's Institute of Kansas City, MO. A fictional diary of a fourteen-year-old victim of incest describing the sequence from disclosure through therapy.

*Feeling Safe Feeling Strong: How to Avoid Sexual Abuse and What to Do If It Happens to You* by Susan Terkel and Janice Rench. Available from Network Publications, Santa Cruz, CA.

*He Told Me Not to Tell* by Jennifer Fay. Available from King County Rape Relief, Renton, WA. A brief but very informative booklet describing sexual abuse and ways of preventing it, written for children age eight and above. An expanded version of this booklet, *No More Secrets* by Caren Adams and Jennifer Fay is available from Network Publications, Santa Cruz, CA.

*It's O.K. to Say NO!* by RGA Publishing Group, Inc., and Frank Smith. Available from Playmore, Inc., Publishers, and Waldman Publishing Corporation, New York, NY. A booklet highlighting the major steps to be taken in preventing sexual abuse, allowing children to color the specific scenes presented. Useful mainly for young children.

*Macho? What Do Girls Really Want?* by Py Bateman and Bill Mahoney. Available from Alternatives to Fear, Seattle, WA. A guide for adolescent boys aiming at developing nonaggressive dating habits.

*The Mouse, the Monster and Me* by Pat Palmer. Available from Impact Publishers in San Luis Obispo, CA. A book intended for young children stressing assertiveness tips, particularly in reaction to unjust or unkind authority.

*My Feelings* by Marsha Morgan. Available from Network Publications, Santa Cruz, CA. A coloring book for children, stressing the private ownership of their bodies and their intuitive feelings about appropriate touches.

*My Very Own Book about Me* by Jo Stowell and Mary Dietzel. Available from Lutheran Social Services in Spokane, WA. A book for both children and adults about basic sexual abuse prevention and various problems in regard to touching.

*My Very Own Special Body Book* by Cary Bassett. Available from Hawthorne Press, Redding, CA. A book designed to be read to children discussing sexual abuse, incest, and methods of prevention and protection.

*Never Say Yes to a Stranger: What Your Child Must Know to Stay Safe* by Susan Newman. Available from Putnam Books in New York, NY. A series of stories designed for parents to read to children describing diverse incidents of sexual abuse by a stranger.

*No More Secrets for Me* by Oralee Wachter. Available from Little, Brown and Company in Boston, MA. A book designed for parents to read to children or for children to read by themselves describing different incidents of sexual abuse.

*Nobody Told Me It Was Rape* by Caren Adams and Jennifer Fay. Available from Network Publications, Santa Cruz, CA. A resource for parents to help them discuss issues concerning acquaintance rape with their adolescent children.

*Rape: What Would You Do If . . . ?* by Dianna Daniels Booher. Available from Julian Mesner Press in New York, NY. A book addressed to adolescent girls describing specific techniques they can use to prevent sexual assault.

*Red Light, Green Light People* by Joy Williams. Available from the Rape and Abuse Crisis Center, Fargo, ND. Coloring book focusing on various types of touches and the feelings they generate, as well as advice on what to do in the case of inappropriate touches.

*Spider Man and Power Pac* by Marvel Comics and the National Committee for Prevention of Child Abuse. Available from Marvel Comics Group in New York, NY. A comic book format describing a sexual abuse situation and what to do if it happens.

*Stop It!* by Eric Berg. Available from Network Publications, Santa Cruz, CA. A booklet for children focusing on their right to say no, containing information about touches, secrets, and personal rights.

*Stories for Free Children* edited by Letty Cottin Pogrevin. Available from McGraw-Hill Publishing Company in New York, NY. A book containing several stories concerning children's rights and freedoms.

*Surviving Sexual Assault* edited by Rachel Grossman and Joan Sutherland. Available from Network Publications, Santa Cruz, CA. A book

designed for crisis-care interviewers (police, emergency room personnel, crisis caseworkers, and so on) in situations of rape and other
sexual assaults.

*Take Care with Yourself* by Laurie White and Steven Spencer. Available from DayStar Press, MI. A book for young children concerning
the basic principles of sexual abuse prevention.

*Tell Someone!* by Eric Berg. Available from Network Publications,
Santa Cruz, CA. A booklet focusing on the idea that sexual abuse is
not the child's fault and that a child should inform if abused.

*Top Secret* by Jennifer Fay and Billie Jo Flerchinger. Available from
King County Rape Relief, Renton, WA. A highly visual and interesting pamphlet written for adolescents and dealing with practical issues
concerning sexual abuse. Contains many personal statements and typical questions posed by teenagers.

*Touch Talk!* by Eric Berg. Available from Network Publications, Santa
Cruz, CA. A booklet about touching to be read to young children in
primary grades.

*Touching* by the Coalition for Child Advocacy. Available from What-
com County Opportunity Council in Bellingham, WA. A storybook
for young children about good and bad touches.

*A Very Touching Book* by Jan Hindman. Available from McClure-
Hindman in Durkee, OR. A book stressing the basic concepts of sexual abuse prevention.

*Why Me? Help for Victims of Child Sexual Abuse (Even If They Are
Adults Now)* by Lynn Daugherty. Available from Network Publications, Santa Cruz, CA. A book covering general issues concerning
sexual abuse and its aftermath, along with first-person stories of victims recounting childhood experiences and specific strategies for helping people cope with victimization.

*The Wonder What Owl* by Jean Mackey and Helen Swan. Available from the Children's Institute of Kansas City, MO. A book to be read to preschool and primary grade children concerning sexual abuse, including specific tips for parents and teachers.

*You Belong to You.* By and available from YWCA Domestic Violence/Sexual Assault Services, Flint, MI. A coloring book for very young children stressing fundamental concepts of self-protection and self-assurance.

# Appendix C:
# Materials for Parents and Trainers

*Alternatives to Fear: A Board Game in Self-Protection.* Available from Alternatives to Fear, Seattle, WA. A game to be used by adolescent and adult women or trainers for sexual offense prevention or crisis situations.

*ANA Family.* Available from West River Sexual Abuse Treatment Center, Child and Family Guidance Services, Rapid City, SD. Anatomically correct dolls for use in prevention programs or interviewing alleged victims of sexual abuse.

*A Better Safe Than Sorry Book* by Sol and Judith Gordon. Available from Network Publications, Santa Cruz, CA. Addressing children ages three to nine, this book contains specific ideas about sexual assault prevention, along with verbatim scripts to be read to children.

*Child/Adult Prevention Principles Series* by Eric Berg. Available from Network Publications, Santa Cruz, CA. A series of short, pocket-size books for children, along with related guides for adults. Useful for children in grades K–6.

*Children Need Protection.* Available from Carver County Program for Victims of Sexual Assault, Chaska, MN. A practical book for parents, including a variety of "what if" and "no" games to play with children.

*Comprehensive K–12 Family Life Curriculum.* Developed by and available from Planned Parenthood of Northern New England, Burlington, VT. A comprehensive curriculum for grades K–12 detailing specific lesson plans on personal safety, decision making, family life, social interaction skills, and self-esteem.

*Happy Bear.* Available from the Kansas Committee for Prevention of Child Abuse, Topeka, KS. A preschool child sexual abuse prevention program intended for children ages three to six.

*How to Take the First Steps* by the staff of Illusion Theater in Minneapolis, MN. Available from Network Publications, Santa Cruz, CA. Discusses larger systems issues regarding community awareness and support, based on the Illusion Theater's extensive sexual abuse prevention program and related plays and programs.

*Intervention with Incestuous Families: A Training Curriculum* by Anne Dorwaldt. Available from Cross Pollination Enterprises Unlimited, Waterbury, VT 05676. Practical training manual with specific lesson plans.

*It's My Body: A Book to Teach Young Children How to Resist Uncomfortable Touch* by Lois Freeman. Available from Network Publications, Santa Cruz, CA. A manual for trainers containing specific ideas and techniques useful in discussing sexual abuse prevention for preschoolers.

*The Key to Having Fun Is Being Safe.* Available from The Safety and Fitness Exchange, Inc., New York, NY. A pamphlet including information about sexual abuse and safety tips for parents to teach children.

*No Easy Answers* by Cordelia Anderson. Available from Network Publications, Santa Cruz, CA. A thorough sexual abuse curriculum (twenty lessons) designed for use in junior and senior high schools. Contains information, topics for discussion, and handouts.

*Personal Safety: Curriculum for Prevention of Child Sexual Abuse* by Marlys Olson. Available from the Child Sexual Abuse Prevention

Program, Tacoma, WA. Comprehensive bibliographic and lesson plan information for all educational levels from preschool through high school.

*Preventing Sexual Abuse: Activities and Strategies for Those Working with Children and Adolescents* by Carol Plummer. Available from Network Publications, Santa Cruz, CA. A set of curriculum guides for grades K–12, containing skeleton outlines of programs for children of different levels.

*Preventing Sexual Abuse: A Newsletter to the National Family Life Education Network.* Available from National Family Life Education Network, Santa Cruz, CA. Quarterly newsletter including new developments in research, resources, and programs in child sexual abuse prevention.

*Safety Kids Set.* Available from Brite Music Enterprises, Inc., Godfrey, IL. A musical approach to teaching children about personal safety.

*Sexual Abuse Prevention: A Study for Teenagers* by Marie Fortune. Available from Network Publications, Santa Cruz, CA. A five-session course for teenagers (ages twelve to eighteen) containing information and topics for discussion.

*Sexual Exploitation: What Parents of Handicapped Persons Should Know.* Available from Seattle Rape Relief Developmental Disabilities Project, Seattle, WA. A brochure aimed at providing information about sexual abuse to parents and special education teachers who deal with handicapped individuals.

*Something Happened to Me* by Phyllis Sweet. Available from Network Publications, Santa Cruz, CA. A training manual emphasizing the use of stories and other techniques to enhance communication.

*Strategies for Free Children: A Leader's Guide to Child Assault Prevention* by Sally Cooper, Yvonne Lutter, and Cathy Phelps. Available from Intrepid Clearing House, Columbus, OH. A self-contained and comprehensive curriculum dealing with general issues of sexual assault and specific strategies aimed at the development of a viable community prevention project.

*Talking about Child Sexual Abuse.* Available from National Committee for Prevention of Child Abuse, Chicago, IL. A comprehensive pamphlet discussing sexual abuse and specific prevention and communication measures.

*Talking to Children/Talking to Parents about Sexual Assault* by Lois Loontjens. Available from Network Publications, Santa Cruz, CA. Specific protocols for talking and teaching about sexual abuse, including exact scripts. This is directed toward adults, but many of the topics can be used by or with children with little modification.

*The Talking and Telling About Touching Game.* Available from Safety Time Games, Akron, OH. A colorful game to be played with young children highlighting prevention techniques.

*Talking about Touching: A Personal Safety Curriculum* by Ruth Harms and Donna James. Available from The Committee for Children, Seattle, WA. One of the best curricula aimed at personal safety, with particular attention paid to touching of various kinds. The information is presented in specific lesson plans, suitable primarily for teachers, counselors, and other child group leaders. This series is available in three grade levels: preschool–K, K–4, and 5–8. Also, there is an associated supplement for physical education teachers and a manual for prevention trainers.

*Teaching Personal Safety Skills: An Implementation Manual* by Anne Dorwaldt. Available from Cross Pollination Enterprises Unlimited, Waterbury, VT 05676. Practical training manual with specific lesson plans.

*Three in Every Classroom: The Child Victim of Incest—What You as a Teacher Can Do* by Ruth Soukup, Sharon Wickner, and Joanne Corbett. Available from Network Publications, Santa Cruz, CA. A manual specifically addressed to teachers, covering all pertinent facts and describing very specific ideas.

*Touch Continuum Study Cards; Touch and Sexual Abuse.* Both available from Network Publications, Santa Cruz, CA. Generated by the Illusion Theater in Minneapolis, this pamphlet and twelve laminated cards provide practical advice and pictorial examples of different kinds of touches.

*What Everyone Should Know about the Sexual Abuse of Children.* Available from Channing L. Bete Co., Inc., South Deerfield, MA. A booklet describing various forms of child sexual abuse, characteristics of offenders, and techniques of prevention.

*Would You Know If Your Child Were Being Sexually Molested?* Available from the Council on Child Sexual Abuse, Tacoma, WA. A pamphlet intended for parents containing a specific script on what to say to a child about various matters connected to child sexual abuse.

# Appendix D:
## Audiovisual Materials

*Best Kept Secret; The Hidden Shame; Every Parent's Nightmare.* Available from Motorola Teleprograms, Inc., Simon & Schuster, Deerfield, IL. Three films produced by ABC's "20/20 News Magazine" containing interviews of parents of children who were sexually exploited in a California preschool, a case of two sisters molested by their father, and several prominent sexual abuse cases along with their legal consequences.

*Better Safe Than Sorry* (I, II, III). Available from Filmfair Communications, Studio City, CA. Three films for different age groups dealing with the dangers of sexual abuse and ways of avoiding it.

*Boys Beware.* Available from DACOM Communications Media, Inc., Glendale, CA. Basic prevention film suitable for adolescents, with specific examples geared to the somewhat different plight of boys versus that of girls.

*Breaking Silence.* Available from Future Educational Films, Inc., Berkeley, CA. A documentary film about incest told by several female and male victims.

*Child Abuse.* Available from the Society for Visual Education, Inc., Chicago, IL. Several filmstrips for teachers, counselors, and students concerning indications of sexual abuse, ways of getting help, and ways of preventing abuse.

*Child Molestation: When to Say No.* Available from Aims Instructional Media Service, Inc., Glendale, CA. Four episodes depicting sexual abuse are presented, with children demonstrating appropriate solutions. Suitable for children over age eight.

*Child Sexual Abuse: The Untold Secret.* Available from the University of Calgary, Calgary, Alberta, Canada. A description of five adolescent victims of incest and their family histories. Suitable for adolescents.

*Child Sexual Abuse: What Your Child Should Know.* Available from Indiana University Audiovisual Center, Bloomington, IN. Originally five television programs for parents and four different age groups produced by WTTW/Chicago detailing information and strategies aimed at preventing child sexual abuse.

*Childhood Sexual Abuse: Four Case Studies.* Available from Motorola Teleprograms, Inc., Simon & Schuster, Deerfield, IL. Four clinical studies aimed at provoking discussion and facilitating in-service training.

*Crime of Silence.* Available from Portia Franklin, New York, NY. Two audiocassettes broadcast on National Public Radio consisting of a four-part series on child sexual abuse.

*Don't Get Stuck There.* Available from Boys Town Center, Boys Town, NE. An instructional film offering advice to adolescents concerning types of abuse and steps to take if abuse occurs. Suitable for adolescents.

*Double Jeopardy.* Available from MTI Teleprograms, Inc., Northbrook, IL. A somewhat critical examination of the frequent systems problems and related insensitivity evident in the investigation of sexual abuse cases. Suitable for parents, teachers, mental health professionals, and other advocates.

*Girls Beware.* Available from DACOM Communications Media, Inc., Glendale, CA. Basic prevention films suitable for adolescents, with specific examples geared to the somewhat different plight of girls versus that of boys.

*If I Tell You a Secret.* Available from Lawren Productions, Mendocino, CA. A film for professionals describing techniques for interviewing sexual abuse victims.

*Incest: The Family Secret.* Available from Filmmakers Library, Inc., New York, NY. Videocassette of women victims discussing their childhood experiences, with particular attention to the role of the mother.

*Incest: The Hidden Crime.* Available from The Media Guild, c/o Association Film, Sun Valley, CA. An excellent documentary depicting a female incest victim and her family, along with practical suggestions about avoiding incest. Suitable for older children and adolescents.

*Incest: The Victim Nobody Believes.* Available from MTI Teleprograms, Inc., Northbrook, IL. A group discussion of three women who were abused as children. Suitable for older children and adolescents.

*Interviewing the Child Abuse Victim.* Available from MTI Teleprograms, Inc., Northbrook, IL. An excellent training resource for professionals depicting different ways of interviewing children who have been physically or sexually abused. Suitable for professionals working directly with children.

*No More Secrets.* Available from ODN Productions, Inc., New York, NY. Nicely presented series of discussions between and among children who reveal sexual abuse episodes they have endured. Suitable for all elementary and middle school children. A sequel (*Talking Helps*) is intended for use by educators, parents, and group leaders.

*Out of the Trap*. Available from the Bridgework Theater, Inc., Goshen, IN. Videotape depicting a sexually exploitive situation, a subsequent discussion about the case, and related information about abuse in general.

*Pedophile*. Available from AIMS Media, Glendale, CA. A film or videocassette describing facts and theories concerning sexual abuse offenders.

*The Safe Child Program—A School Curriculum*. Available from Health Education Systems, Inc., New York, NY. A series of videotapes on different aspects of personal safety.

*Sexual Abuse: The Family*. Available from National Audio-Visual Center, Washington, D.C. A general overview of sexual abuse within the family, stressing medical aspects and role playing. Suitable for professionals working directly with children, especially professionals in health care.

*Shatter the Silence*. Available from S-L Film Productions, Los Angeles, CA. A dramatic portrayal of the adolescence and young adulthood experiences of a female incest victim. Suitable for adolescents.

*Speak Up, Say No!* Available from Krause House, Oregon City, OR. Cartoon-oriented format using animal characters (mice) depicting a sexual abuse incident. Suitable for preschoolers (ages three to six).

*Strong Kids, Safe Kids*. Available from Paramount Studios, Hollywood, CA. A videocassette featuring Henry Winkler, John Ritter, and Mariette Hartley presenting different abusive situations.

*Targets*. Available from Motorola Teleprograms, Inc., Simon & Schuster, Deerfield, IL. Film intended for teenagers describing ways of avoiding victimization in several contexts.

*A Time for Caring: The School's Response to the Sexually Abused Child.* Available from Lawren Productions, Inc., Los Angeles, CA. An excellent film focusing on indications of sexual abuse and techniques school personnel can use to help abused children. Suitable for teachers and other helping professionals. A companion film (*The Sexually Abused Child*) provides a model for handling child sexual abuse cases at different levels of the criminal justice system.

*What Tadoo.* Available from Motorola Teleprograms, Inc., Simon & Schuster, Deerfield, IL. An appealing film intended for young children stressing three alternative approaches to prevention of sexual abuse, featuring a delightful cast of puppets from the Land of Listen.

*Who Do You Tell?* Available from MTI Teleprograms, Inc., Northbrook, IL. A film stressing the role of supportive adults in a variety of dangerous or threatening situations. Suitable for young children (ages five to ten).

# References

Adams, Caren, and Jennifer Fay. 1981. *No More Secrets: Protecting Your Child from Sexual Assault*. San Luis Obispo, CA: Impact Publishers.

Armstrong, L. 1978. *Kiss Daddy Goodnight: A Speak-Out on Incest*. New York: Hawthorne.

Brownmiller, Susan. 1975. *Against Our Will: Men, Women and Rape*. New York: Simon and Schuster.

Burgess, A., N. Groth, L. Holstrom, and S. Sgroi. 1978. *Sexual Assault of Children and Adolescents*. Lexington, MA: Lexington Books.

Butler, Sandra. 1978. *Conspiracy of Silence: The Trauma of Incest*. San Francisco: New Glide Publications.

Finkelhor, David. 1984. *Child Sexual Abuse: New Theory and Research*. New York: Free Press.

Forward, Susan. 1978. *Betrayal of Innocence: Incest and Its Devastation*. East Rutherford, NJ: Penguin Books.

Freeman-Longo, Robert E. 1985. "The Adolescent Sexual Offender: Background and Research Perspectives." In *Adolescent Sex Offenders: Issues in Research and Treatment* (Otey, Emeline M. and Gail D. Ryan, editors), Rockville, MD: U.S. Department of Health and Human Services.

Geiser, Robert L. 1979. *Hidden Victims: The Sexual Abuse of Children*. Boston: Beacon Press.

Goldstein, Seth L. 1987. *The Sexual Exploitation of Children: A Practical Guide to Assessment, Investigation, and Intervention*. New York: Elsevier Science Publishing Company.

Groth, Nicholas. 1979. *Men Who Rape*. New York: Plenum.

Herman, Judith. 1981. *Father-Daughter Incest*. Cambridge, MA: Harvard University Press.

James, Beverly, and Maria Nasjleti. 1983. *Treating Sexually Abused Children and Their Families*. Palo Alto, CA: Consulting Psychologists Press.

Justice, Blair, and Rita Justice. 1979. *The Broken Taboo*. New York: Human Sciences Press.

Kempe, Ruth S., and C. Henry Kempe. 1984. *The Common Secret: Sexual Abuse of Children and Adolescents*. New York: W.H. Freeman & Co.

L'Abate, Luciano, editor. 1985. *The Handbook of Family Psychology and Therapy.* Homewood, IL: Dorsey Press.

MacFarlane, Kee, and Jill Waterman, editors. 1986. *Sexual Abuse of Young Children.* New York: Guilford.

Mayer, Adele. 1983. *Incest: A Treatment Manual for Therapy with Victims, Spouses and Offenders.* Holmes Beach, FL: Learning Publications.

Meiselman, Karin. 1978. *Incest: A Psychological Study of Causes and Effects with Treatment Recommendations.* San Francisco: Jossey-Bass.

Mrazek, Patricia Beezley, and C. Henry Kempe, editors. 1981. *Sexually Abused Children and Their Families.* New York: Pergamon Press.

Nabokov, Vladimir. 1955. *Lolita.* New York: Putnam.

National Center on Child Abuse and Neglect. U.S. Department of Health and Human Services. *Sexual Abuse of Children: Selected Readings.* Washington, DC: Government Printing Office.

Nurcombe, Barry. 1983. "Child Credibility,." Unpublished paper, now at Emma Pendleton Bradley Hospital, Providence, RI.

Rush, Florence. 1980. *The Best Kept Secret: Sexual Abuse of Children.* New York: McGraw-Hill.

Russell, Diana E. 1986. *The Secret Trauma: Incest in the Lives of Girls and Women.* New York: Basic Books.

Sanford, Linda. 1980. *The Silent Children.* New York: Doubleday.

Sgroi, Suzanne M., editor. 1982. *Handbook of Clinical Intervention in Child Sexual Abuse.* Lexington, MA: D.C. Heath.

Walters, David R. 1975. *Physical and Sexual Abuse of Children: Causes and Treatment.* Bloomington, IN: Indiana University Press.

# Index

# About the Authors

DONALD HILLMAN, PH.D., is a Clinical Associate Professor of Psychiatry at the University of Vermont, where he engages in teaching, consultation, research, and clinical practice. He has a doctorate in psychology from Harvard University and did his formal clinical internship at The Texas Institute for Research Sciences in Houston. He is licensed as a psychologist in Vermont and is on The National Register of Health Service Providers in Psychology. He recently received The Commissioner's Award from the State of Vermont for outstanding services to the welfare of Vermont children. Together with Janice Solek-Tefft, he has been active on committees and groups dealing with child sexual abuse and has evaluated and treated many cases involving sexual abuse.

JANICE L. SOLEK-TEFFT, M.A., received a B.F.A. from Kent State University and an M.A. in Art Therapy from Goddard College. She is a Certified Guidance Counselor and Art Therapist. She has provided training and led discussions for parents, psychologists, psychotherapists, social workers, physicians and lawyers regarding the sexual abuse and neglect of children and the impact it has had on their art productions. She is currently a Guidance Counselor for elementary aged children in grades K–4 and a psychotherapist in private practice. Both she and Donald Hillman are members of the Child Sexual Abuse Response Team in the State of Vermont.